Evaluating the
Whole Curriculum

Evaluating the Whole Curriculum

Jon Nixon

OPEN UNIVERSITY PRESS
Milton Keynes · Philadelphia

Open University Press
Celtic Court
22 Ballmoor
Buckingham
MK18 1XW

and

1900 Frost Road, Suite 101
Bristol, PA 19007, USA

First Published 1992

British Library Cataloguing in Publication Data

Evaluating the whole curriculum.
– (SRHE/Open University Press series)
I. Nixon, Jon   II. Series
373.19

ISBN 0–335–09457–0 (hb)
ISBN 0–335–09456–2 (pb)

Library of Congress Cataloging-in-Publication Data

Nixon, Jon.
Evaluating the whole curriculum / Jon Nixon.
p.   cm.
Includes bibliographical references (p.   ) and index.
ISBN 0–335–09457–0 – ISBN 0–335–09456–2 (pbk.)
1. Educational evaluation—Great Britain.   I. Title.
LB2822.75.N59   1991
375′.006′0941—dc20   91–21242 CIP

Typeset by Colset Private Limited, Singapore
Printed and bound in Great Britain by J.W. Arrowsmith Limited, Bristol

*For Elizabeth
in love and solidarity*

Human beings should meet together, not to enforce, but to enquire.
(*William Godwin, 1793*)

I wish, first, that we should recognise that education is ordinary: that it is, before everything else, the process of giving to the ordinary members of society its full common meanings, and the skills that will enable them to amend these meanings, in the light of their personal and common experience.
(*Raymond Williams, 1958*)

Criticism is a matter of looking on this picture and on that, not of comparing both pictures with the original. Nothing can serve as a criticism of a person save another person, or of a culture save an alternative culture.
(*Richard Rorty, 1989*)

Contents

Preface and Acknowledgements xi
Abbreviations xiii

1 Accountability and Control 1
2 Why Evaluate? 20
3 A Formative Process 36
4 The Whole Curriculum 51
5 Outcome Measures 71
6 Interview Evidence 87
7 The Knowable Community 101
8 Beyond the Secret Garden 116

Bibliography 128
Index 139

Preface and Acknowledgements

Ten years ago I edited a book entitled *A Teachers' Guide to Action Research*, which focused on the notion of teachers as evaluators of their own practice. In some ways this book revisits that old territory. In other ways, of course, that territory is part of a past country: all the old sites have been changed. The school and LEA in which I was working at the time no longer exist (the one amalgamated into non-existence, the other disbanded); the curriculum I taught across has been rationalized into the tidy confines of the National Curriculum; the curriculum areas I taught within – and wrote about – have become marginalized, recategorized or simply obliterated. The colleagues I worked with have moved on, or out, many of them no longer involved in the everyday running of schools. Those that remain struggle with the intricacies of local financial management and await, with varying degrees of trepidation, the introduction of an unwieldy system of standardized assessment.

Evaluation has come to mean something different over the last ten years and has been differently interpreted by different groups. For central government departments and agencies it has become associated with the search for often crude and trivializing performance indicators. For LEAs it has meant the introduction of contracted or seconded local evaluators, often ill equipped for, and unskilled in, the tricky task of evaluation. For schools, however, which are willing to adopt a self-critical and explorative enquiry into the values underlying their own practice, it can remain an important act of self-determination. Agency, conceived as a corporate and reflective endeavour, is a cornerstone of the approach to educational evaluation outlined within this book.

The 1980s – for this writer at least – have been marked by contradictions. Almost every major initiative with which as an evaluator I have been associated has originated from, or been supported by, a government which has been characterized by its insensitivity to the age-old aspirations of a liberalizing education. Yet education – not only in spite of, but through those same initiatives – has continued to liberalize: to challenge the narrow, restrictive notion of 'vocational', to insist that in-service education is more than just skills training and to assert that low attainment is an institutional as well as an individual phenomenon. The contradictions have – always – to be thought through, worried over, worked on. But they can be countered.

Thanks to the editors of *British Journal of Educational Studies*, *Evaluation and Research in Education*, *Journal of Curriculum Studies* and *Westminster Studies in Education* for allowing me a preliminary sketch of some of the ideas that are developed on the broader canvas afforded by this publication. Thanks also to Jean Rudduck for her intellectual generosity and professional support over the last ten years, to Wilf Carr for the continuing fraternal dialogue, and to all my colleagues at QQSE for helping to create a context in which ideas matter. Finally, thanks to Elizabeth O'Brien – friend, wife and colleague – for challenging the old presuppositions and for enduring the inroads that the production of this public statement has made into our own private space.

The limitations and shortcomings of this book remain, of course, entirely my own responsibility.

Jon Nixon

Abbreviations

AMMA	Assistant Masters and Mistressess Association
BEMAS	British Educational Management and Administration Society
CCCS	Centre for Contemporary Cultural Studies, University of Birmingham
CPVE	Certificate of Pre-Vocational Education
DES	Department of Education and Science
DTI	Department of Trade and Industry
EEA	Educating for Economic Awareness Project
ERA	Education Reform Act (1988)
GCSE	General Certificate of Secondary Education
HMI	Her Majesty's Inspectorate
ILEA	Inner London Education Authority
INSET	In-Service Education and Training
LAPP	Lower Attaining Pupils Programme
LEA	Local Education Authority
LMS	Local Management of Schools
MSC	Manpower Services Commission (now TA)
NCC	National Curriculum Council
SATs	Standard Assessment Tasks
SCIA	Society of Chief Inspectors and Advisers
SCIP	School Curriculum Industry Partnership
TA	Training Agency (formerly MSC)
TGAT	Task Group on Assessment and Testing

TRIST   TVEI-Related In-Service Training Scheme
TVEI   Technical and Vocational Education Initiative

– 1 –

Accountability and Control

Evaluation, as an attempt to understand and thereby improve educational practice, is highly susceptible to changes in the political climate. Over the last ten years, in particular, those involved in educational evaluation have had to accommodate themselves to shifts of policy and principle that have wide ranging implications for the way in which evaluation is conducted and perceived. In order to consider the role that evaluation might play within the education system of the 1990s, it is therefore important to track those shifts and so gain a clearer sense of what educational evaluation has become over the last decade. What use schools are able to make of evaluation in the future will depend largely on the quality of the evaluative traditions and practices that are handed down to them.

A backward glance

The last ten years have seen unprecedented changes in the education service. Successive waves of government legislation have radically altered the constitution of school governing bodies, the authority of local government in respect of school funding and finance, and the responsibility of schools – and by implication teachers – for determining the form and content of their curricula. These changes signify an historic shift in the traditional power relation between central government, LEAs and that diverse professional grouping which includes teachers, headteachers and those who –

in either an in-service or administrative capacity – support them.

There can be no doubt about the direction of that shift. What has been, and is continually, questioned, however, is the interpretation that should be placed on it. Was it, as central government would claim, an attempt to break the hegemonic control of the professionals: an allocation of power to the people? Or was it, rather, a ploy to consolidate power: an attempt at centrally imposed curriculum control by a cabinet of which the vast majority of members had no direct experience, as pupils, parents or teachers, of the state education system? Either way Thatcherism changed the face of British schooling, not least by placing it as a major item on the agenda of public and political debate.

A key strategy for effecting these changes has been the use of categorical funding programmes, whereby – through managing agents such as the TA or DES – central government has been able to define and prioritize key categories of spending within the education sector. Thus, programmes such as the TVEI pilot, TRIST, LAPP and, more recently, the TVEI national extension have not only been mechanisms for dispensing public funds; they have also proved to be a powerful means of controlling the kinds of curriculum development and in-service education that are on offer. This funding strategy may in retrospect be seen to have had as great an influence on schooling as the more obvious, and more earnestly contested, introduction of the National Curriculum. Certainly, the latter would have been even more difficult to implement than it already is were it not for those earlier initiatives. For in many ways they prepared the ground for the more extensive centralized control assumed through the Education Reform Act of 1988.

Under the new dispensation there has, of course, been an increased emphasis on the vocational and applied aspects of learning. Initially, this emphasis often meant little more than the introduction of a series of discrete curriculum units targeted at groups of students categorized as academically less able. More recently, however, its relevance for all pupils has been realized, with economic and industrial understanding having been defined by the NCC as one of five major cross-curricular themes within the National Curriculum (NCC 1989). Critics of the various government inspired initiatives that have fostered the new vocationalism point to its instrumentalism and evident reliance on what they see as a crude means/end model of learning. (See for example, Cohen 1984 and Chitty 1986.) Those more sympathetic to the centralizing tendencies of these initiatives view it as a necessary means of quality control.

My own view is that initiatives such as TVEI, while undoubtedly skewing the educational agenda towards a vocationally oriented government priority, have in some circumstances enabled teachers to promote liberal values and to adopt many of the inquiry based approaches to learning that have developed over the past twenty years. Those initiatives can constitute, in other words (as I have argued elsewhere) 'a shady space in which radical practice can flourish in relative obscurity' (Clough and Nixon 1989). Nevertheless, the parameters are clearly set. What space there is for wary experimentalism and reflective practice by teachers has been hard won and is by no means securely held.

For teachers were, as an occupational group, systematically shorn of their curriculum and pedagogical autonomy throughout the 1980s. Traditionally that autonomy had been the cornerstone of the particular version of professionalism adopted by teachers. With that version, as Gerald Grace points out, they 'had fought off the impositions of payment by results in the nineteenth century and they had also fought off accusations of indoctrination and political bias in the 20's'. It might reasonably be expected, therefore, that they would successfully fight off the reassertion of explicit state control in the 1980s by similar means. After all,

> the whole historical consciousness and experience of organised teachers suggested that in the face of central state initiatives this version of professionalism would be their best defence.
>
> (Grace 1987: 220)

This, however, was to reckon without the crisis of confidence within the professions generally (as analysed, for example, in Schön 1987) and the strategic use of that crisis by central government. Characterized as out of touch with both productive industry and parental expectations, teachers became an easy scapegoat for the economic failures of the 1970s. The charges levelled against them – incompetence, slovenliness, political bias, anti-authoritarianism – have provided a simple and ready made explanation of Britain's contemporary social and economic ills. From that populist perspective, the 'control of teachers, of curriculum and of standards had been lost by the excessive development of principles of teacher autonomy' (Grace 1987: 216). The answers to the contemporary problems of state schooling could, from that same perspective, be found only in a reassertion of centralized control over both the curriculum and the procedures of teaching and learning.

The year long dispute of 1985–86 made that task of reassertion considerably easier than it might otherwise have been. The disruptions of this period greatly increased public anxiety about local government competence in the management of schools, about the 'professional commitment' and 'dedication' of teachers and about the extent to which teachers as a group could speak with a unified and authoritative voice. Given the narrow trade union approach adopted, teachers failed to communicate the educational successes of the post-war era as evidenced, for example, in the steady increase of school-leavers obtaining qualifications and the general reduction in social class segregation. The possibility of effective future resistance to the Education Reform Act of 1988 was thereby weakened by the choice of what Michael Rustin refers to as the 'tactics of maximum disruption at minimum cost over a serious attempt to mobilise parents, schoolchildren and communities on a populist basis' (1989: 71).

Ironically, it was within this period that educational evaluation underwent something of a renaissance. For in many of the programmes developed during the mid-1980s a condition laid upon LEAs by funding bodies was that some form of local evaluation be conducted. Moreover, these programmes were usually also evaluated at the national level. As a result, therefore, an upsurge in evaluation activities, involving a wide range of professional expertise, has taken place at all levels of the education system: from teachers concerned with evaluating their own classroom practice through to contracted (often university based) evaluators focusing upon the broader aspects of policy development.

The emergent paradigm

Within this context evaluation can be categorized somewhat crudely in terms of a continuum, with the measurement of quantifiable data at one extreme and naturalistic description of complex social settings at the other. Along the continuum approaches can be distinguished in terms of the data drawn on, the data collection techniques employed and the kinds of reporting that result.

The limitations of the notion of evaluation-as-measurement are now well documented and widely accepted, Hamilton *et al.* 1977.

Such a conception presupposes the possibility of determining base-lines and indices, of isolating variables and developing appropriate instruments; and each of these activities becomes highly problematic in situations where change is both rapid and varied. Given the many strategic interventions that are likely to be undertaken, baselines become blurred and variables shift between cases. Moreover, there may be serious differences of opinion between those involved regarding what constitutes change and how it should be measured. These limitations, as Malcolm Parlett and David Hamilton have pointed out, suggest that applying this evaluation approach 'to the study of innovations is often a cumbersome and inadequate procedure' (1977: 9).

Those approaches at the other end of the continuum which seek to provide naturalistic description avoid many of these limitations. Indeed, their development has in many cases been prompted by a reaction against the reductionism of the more positivist aspects of the evaluation-as-measurement paradigm, together with a recognition of the need for alternative ways of seeing 'the complexities and richness of educational life' (Eisner 1985: 140). Such approaches raise their own problems, however, particularly when viewed in the context of school focused curriculum innovation. For to describe changing social structures in such a way as to reflect their salient and idiosyncratic features is an immensely time consuming task, in terms of both data collection and clearance. And time, for those who are caught up in the process of curriculum change, is always in short supply.

Nevertheless, the emphasis on holistic enquiry has been extremely influential, not only in the field of education, but across a wide range of intellectual disciplines. In cultural and literary theory, for example, the work of Raymond Williams has lent enormous intellectual weight to the view that the study of art works and forms is necessarily 'the study of relations between elements in a whole way of life'; that it must be informed, in other words, by a 'theory of social totality' (1980: 20). Similarly, John Berger (particularly in his fruitful collaboration with the photographer Jean Mohr) shows how visual images, story and interview can complement one another 'so as not only to illustrate, but also to articulate a lived experience' (1982: 134); that of an English doctor, for example, or a migrant worker in Europe, or a French peasant woman (1969; 1975; 1982).

Neither of these two writers has necessarily had a *direct* influence on educational evaluation (though in certain instances they may well have done). Their work (and the work of others writing within this tradition) has, however, helped to create an intellectual climate conducive to complex naturalistic modes of enquiry and, as such, has undoubtedly exerted considerable *indirect* influence on the way in which evaluation has been conducted. Moreover, it points to a general movement of ideas whereby many of the positivist assumptions underlying more traditional social scientific approaches came to be viewed with increasing scepticism. It is within this general movement that the more specific developments we are discussing within curriculum evaluation need to be located.

Viewed historically, then, the drift from measurement to rich description represents a fundamental paradigm shift to which the style of evaluation that is now gaining dominance within educational circles can be seen as a significant response. That style owes something to the reconceptualization of research and evaluation as achieved within those approaches located more towards the descriptive end of the continuum. It is, however, a distinctive style, independent of this earlier orientation and with its own characteristics and antecedents. What we are faced with is a real change in what is conceived of as the nature and purpose of educational evaluation.

The prime purpose of evaluation, as framed by the emergent paradigm, is to inform the immediate decisions of policy makers and practitioners. In this respect it differs significantly from those styles of evaluation at the descriptive end of the continuum, the main aim of which was to aid reflection rather than action. Unlike those at the measurement end, however, it fulfils its purpose by highlighting issues implicit in the process of curriculum development. It attempts, in other words, to be both user focused (in terms of its orientation towards specific outcomes) and process oriented (in terms of its focus on particular contexts).

A further aspect of the emergent paradigm is its emphasis on the role of the teacher within the evaluation process. Throughout the late 1960s and early 1970s a number of projects began to define a stronger role for teachers in curriculum evaluation and development. These projects were funded in the main by the then Schools Council, but also to a lesser extent by the Nuffield and Ford Foundations and by a number of professional associations. Characterized by their large-scale structure and their emphasis on implementation through the development of teaching materials, several of them did nevertheless seek to involve teachers in the process of development, diffusion and (later and to a lesser extent) classroom research.

Lawrence Stenhouse, drawing primarily on his experience of directing the Humanities Curriculum Project, typified this role as 'the teacher as researcher'. In a much quoted passage, he defined its major characteristics as being 'a capacity for autonomous professional self-development through systematic self-study, through the study of the work of other teachers and through the testing of ideas by classroom research procedures' (1975: 144). Although rarely alluded to by Stenhouse, there was a precedent for this reformulation in work carried out in America by Stephen Corey (1953) and Abraham Shumsky (1956; 1958). John Elliott drew more explicitly on this earlier American tradition of action research, both in his direction of the Ford Teaching Project (1975) and in his later coordination of the Classroom Action Research Network based at the Cambridge Institute of Education. The latter, though by no means extensive in its membership, was significant in that it attempted to offer a framework whereby teachers involved in classroom research and evaluation could communicate across institutional and geographical boundaries. It sought, in other words, to establish a research community centred on the concerns of practising teachers.

As an aspiration at least, the notion of 'the teacher as researcher' has survived in many of the more progressive aspects of current educational practice: the emphasis on the *ownership* of change, the increased *participation* of teachers in the process of local and school-based evaluation and the heavy premium placed on *partnership*: see for example, Nixon 1987; Rudduck and Wilcox 1988. If that notion now seems somewhat dated, it is because the political climate (under the influence of a central government which has assumed a mandate for a radical overhaul of the education system as a whole) has changed rapidly throughout the 1980s. As Rob Walker foresaw at the outset of the decade, the dominant trend has been the 'growing separation between the worlds of controllers and controlled throughout the education system' (1980: 51).

The full impact of this separation, as far as curriculum evaluation is concerned, cannot as yet be gauged. What is certain, however, is that the widespread educational changes that have occasioned the separation are major determinants of the new styles of evaluation emerging within the present context. Those responsible for evaluating the school curriculum cannot afford to relinquish the earlier focus upon the *processes* of classroom interaction; but nor can they ignore the increasing stress placed upon the measurement of pre-specified *outcomes*. What is required is an approach to evaluation that is sensitive to that previous tradition and at the same time robust enough to respond to the heavy accountability demands currently being made upon schools. With the National Curriculum established (though its full implementation stretches through to 1997), there will, it is hoped, now be an opportunity for teachers to appropriate the emergent paradigm and shape its development according to their own professional needs and values.

Mechanisms of accountability

In fulfilling that role teachers will need to square up to changed circumstances and acknowledge the extent to which, and mechanisms by which, public accountability now determines the work of schools and, indeed, the ways in which schools judge their own effectiveness. The Education Reform Act (1988) is a key reference point in tracking these changes and it should be borne in mind that, though that piece of legislation is usually associated with the National Curriculum, it is in fact something of a hotchpotch, dealing as it does with admissions procedures, finance and staffing, opting out arrangements as well as the reorganization and funding of higher education and the dismantling of the ILEA. Moreover, it builds on the earlier (1986) Education Act, which within its own strange miscellany of provision included the enabling legislation whereby appraisal schemes were to be imposed on teachers if this became necessary. The implementation of the National Curriculum and its evaluation by schools must be viewed in the context of this broader apparatus of control.

Schools in the market-place

Some of the less accessible sections of the 1988 Act are those dealing with the arrangements for the admission of pupils to state schools. Section 26 (1) informs us that those arrangements shall not be such as to 'fix as the number of pupils in any relevant age group it is intended to admit to the school in any school year a number which is less than the relevant standard number'. Not until the following section of the Act are we informed that the 'relevant standard number' must be higher than the number of pupils entering the school in the year preceding the Act's implementation (the 'pre-commencement number', to employ the terminology of the Act). This means in effect that one of the main grounds upon which LEAs were (under the terms of the 1980 Act) able to exercise the right to refuse compliance with parental preference as to the school at which their child should be educated has been withdrawn.

Schools, then, have been pushed towards expansionism; particularly so since their level of funding (under Section 38 (3) of the 1988 Act) is dependent upon their success in this entrepreneurial venture. Coordinated planning across a community of schools regarding levels of intake, mutual support with regard to the allocation of resources, and the development of specialist centres of expertise within particular institutions has thereby been made that much more difficult. Moreover, the possibility of schools opting out of LEA control altogether (Section 60) increases the likelihood of competition between schools and this, ultimately, can only serve to sharpen the inequalities within the education service as a whole.

There would seem to be a fundamental contradiction in the system at this point. Given that LEA advisory services, which have traditionally carried a weighty INSET brief, are being pushed towards an increasingly inspectorial role in respect of schools' delivery of the National Curriculum, each school has now to shoulder a much heavier burden of responsibility regarding the professional development of its own staff. Since, however, schools are now, as a result of LMS (see Coopers and Lybrand 1988), much more self-dependent in terms of the management of their own financial resources, they are less likely to share those resources for the purposes of INSET provision. While in the past seconded advisory teachers might have been expected to fulfil a key role in cross-school staff development, schools are now understandably less willing to drain their scant resources in this way. The 1988 Act has, therefore, created an INSET vacuum which is likely to have serious repercussions for the continuation of effective staff development generally and school-based evaluation in particular.

In many localities schools are successfully resisting the pull of this particular version of the enterprise culture: older loyalties survive, with the result that schools continue to work together, drawing on the kinds of consortia arrangements that, ironically, were originally established under central government funding (TRIST 1987; Bridgewood 1989). In-school evaluation within this scenario is necessarily tied to the processes of public accountability. It can also function, however, as a means of helping the institution understand its particular strengths and to articulate these fully for the purpose of communicating more directly with parents and neighbouring schools. Under the terms of the 1988 Act, schools are undeniably in the market-place; but evaluation can at least help them to ensure that they bring their own principled value stance to bear on the transactions.

Assessing, recording and reporting

By 1997 the National Curriculum will have achieved its apotheosis with the first reported assessment of modern languages at Key Stage 4. Prior to this, in clearly defined stages, the introduction and assessment of the other foundation subjects will have slotted into place. There is, of course, the very real possibility that by that time the entire structure will be groaning under the bureaucratic weight of its own assessment procedures. Nevertheless, it must be acknowledged that (regardless, I think, of any electoral changes in the interim) the National Curriculum, together with the assessment and testing arrangements accompanying it, are here to stay in some form or other for some considerable time.

Since the particular assessment tasks to be used are still being devised, it is difficult to comment on them in any detail. On the evidence of the Key Stage 1 materials that are available, it is possible, however, to be cautiously optimistic that the advice of the Task Group on Assessment and Testing will be heeded at least in respect of the desirability of using 'a mixture of standardised assessment instruments including tests, practical tasks and observations' and of including 'teachers' ratings of pupil performance . . . as a fundamental element of the national assessment system' (DES 1988a: 227). In other words, that system may well not be quite as crude as was at first feared. Even so it is difficult not to sympathize with the view that

> the detail of the testing programme is unimportant compared to the overarching themes of the Act as a whole . . . permeated (as it is) by notions of competition, of external, centralised control, of selection and of systems accountability.
>
> (Clough and Clough 1989: 29–30)

What is particularly worrying is that the proposed assessment programme may well put at risk some of the more innovative and far reaching developments of the past decade at the very time when they are beginning to make a real impact. Most schools, for example, have now extended the range of what they assess, and how, by providing CPVE or similar pre-vocational courses. Many have also become caught up in profiling either as single institutions or as members of a consortium of schools. Among the more ambitious cross-LEA consortia schemes are the Oxford Certificate of Educational Achievement and the Northern Partnership for Records of Achievement, both of which are designed to provide examination board accreditation for the recorded achievement of individual pupils. The profiling element of TVEI has also proved influential in this respect (TVEI 1988). Even in those schools that have remained largely immune to these more progressive influences, the demands of GCSE are being felt as a requirement laid upon all teachers to identify detailed criteria for each aspect of their subject and to use these for the purpose of regular coursework assessment.

Each of these developments has placed a strong emphasis on the need 'to organise teaching in such a way that assessment is an integral part of it and not a bolt-on activity' (Broadfoot 1990: 654). More specifically, and with varying degrees of emphasis, they have all focused on the role of the pupil within the assessment process and on enlarging the criteria of educational success so as to recognize a broader range of pupil achievement. It is still unclear as to how, if at all, these emphases will figure in the assessment of the National Curriculum. As yet there seem to be few signs that pupil self-assessment will form a significant part of the new system or that competitive selection will give way to positive achievement as the conceptual cornerstone. Indeed, what seems much more likely is that the 'the attempt to make assessment serve the learning process will be rendered impotent by the lack of trust which imposes external criteria for judgement on schools and teachers' (Broadfoot 1988: 18).

Whatever form the final assessment procedures take they will undoubtedly betoken a shift of focus away from the individual student (as in records of achievement) and towards the accountability of systems (whether these be individual schools or LEAs.) Within this kind of climate, evaluation will, of course, need to utilize the progressively accumulating data source produced as a result of national testing at the end of each of the key stages. More importantly, however, it will have a significant role in ensuring that the results of assessment tasks are fully contextualized and carefully balanced against other kinds of data. Simply because the output data will be available in such rich abundance, there will be an increasing tendency to over-rely upon it. The right kind of approach to evaluation can serve to remind us that 'raw measures of outcome (e.g. SATs) will say very little about the achievement of schools unless carefully qualified and contextualised' (SCIA 1989: 3).

Teacher appraisal

As long ago as 1983 Sir Keith Joseph, then Secretary of State for Education, was arguing that those managing schools had 'a clear responsibility to establish, in consultation with their teachers, a policy for staff deployment and training based on a systematic assessment of every teacher's performance' (DES 1983: 27). Developing this theme at two successive North of England Education Conferences (Joseph 1984; 1985), he thereby laid the foundations for what has been called 'the Government's managerialist strategy for developing the statutory phase of schooling' (Wilcox 1986: 1). In 1985 the White Paper *Better Schools* built upon this foundation by relating appraisal directly to pay, responsibilities and performance. Thereafter there could be little doubt that teacher appraisal was to be 'seen as the key instrument for managing this relationship, with teachers' . . . salary progression largely determined by reference to periodic assessment of performance' (DES 1985a: 55–6).

What doubt remained was soon dispelled by the 1986 Education Act which was piloted through parliament by Kenneth Baker, successor to Keith Joseph as Secretary of State for Education. That legislation was later embodied in *The Education (School Teachers' Pay and Conditions of Employment) Order 1987*, which imposed detailed conditions of service on the teaching profession; including (for headteachers) 'supervising and participating in any arrangements within an agreed national framework for the appraisal of the performance of teachers' and (for all other teachers) 'participating in any arrangements within an agreed national framework for the appraisal of his performance and that of other teachers'.

Against this background six pilot appraisal projects were established in Croydon, Cumbria, Newcastle-upon-Tyne, Salford, Somerset and Suffolk. The progress of these six projects was monitored by a National Steering Group comprising representatives of the DES, local authorities' associations and the teachers' unions. Its report, published by the DES in October 1989, put forward agreed recommendations on a national framework for appraisal and, as

Alan Evans (vice-chairman of the National Steering Group) put it, represented a victory for those who have argued that 'teacher appraisal . . . will only improve teaching and learning if it is a professional process trusted by teachers' (Evans 1989). On the day that this report was published, Kenneth Baker's successor John MacGregor announced that he would not immediately be drawing up regulations based on the National Steering Group's recommendations. Instead, he would be inviting comments on those proposals and intended to produce guidance in mid-1990.

These consultations were overtaken by political events when, in the autumn of 1990, Kenneth Clarke was appointed Secretary of State for Education. One of his first announcements on taking office was that teacher appraisal would follow a regular two-year cycle and that 'its main features will be an observation by a senior colleague of the teaching work in the classroom, to be followed by an interview in which the appraiser will discuss the appraisee's professional development with him'. The Secretary of State also maintained that 'disciplinary procedures . . . may draw on appraisal records' and that head teachers will be able to draw on information from appraisal 'in advising governing bodies on the exercise of their responsibilities for remuneration'. (Clarke 1990).

Four Secretaries of State later, the question of what exactly is meant by teacher appraisal remains, therefore, largely unresolved. Les Bell has suggested that there are in fact six 'sets of meanings which have exerted a considerable influence over staff attitudes to appraisal processes in schools in recent years'. These he summarizes as follows (1988: 9–16):

1 identifying incompetent teachers;
2 improving pay and promotions;
3 external accountability;
4 improving teacher performance;
5 effective management of teachers;
6 professional development.

The earlier statements by Keith Joseph (1984; 1985) and the DES (1983; 1985a; 1985b) clearly embodied the first three sets of meanings. Even when (as in Bell's fourth and fifth categories) teacher appraisal has been associated with school improvement, rather than the drive towards accountability, it has nevertheless contained an implicitly deficit model of teachers (although the emphasis on incompetence is often softened by a general reference to demoralization). As for any suggestion that teachers might take responsibility for, and control of, their own professional development (Bell's sixth category), there is little evidence that this figures significantly in the thinking of either central government or LEAs. At best, it would seem, 'the person being managed is entitled to know what the organisation goals are . . . (and) how successfully he or she contributed to the achievement of those goals' (Trethowan 1987: 1). This is a poor substitute for the full, active engagement by teachers in the improvement, and understanding, of their own professional practice.

The 'performance indicator' debate

The current concern with value for money, pupil achievement measures and teacher effectiveness finds a somewhat obsessive focus in the debate on performance indicators. No one, to be honest, seems at all clear about what exactly a performance indicator is (Harland and Sumner 1989: 12). Nevertheless, the idea – with its misleading promise of an infallible yardstick by which schools might be judged – carries considerable attraction, especially among those who choose to remain conveniently unaware of the extent to which those judgements are necessarily dependent upon the particularities of the school setting.

It is important to bear in mind, therefore, that performance indicators are at best 'signposts and markers' (CIPFA 1986) and that, as such, 'they are part of a process which is much more important than the indicators themselves' (Tipple 1989: 281); a process, that is, of consultation whereby schools articulate for themselves and others what they consider to be a good standard of performance or appropriate achievement in a particular field. As the Society of Chief Inspectors and Advisers rightly points out,

> much of what has passed, in the recent debate, as performance indicator material has been flawed by its tendency to amass the totality of data which can be applied to a school, without focus or discrimination.
>
> (SCIA 1989: 4)

It has failed, in other words, to generate the systematic application of judgement that ought to be its prime aim.

One reason for this failure has been the tendency to over-emphasize quantifiable indicators, particularly those which provide a measure of outcome. As the DES itself acknowledges, 'a major deficiency is that the outcome measures currently available are limited to those based on examination achievements' (DES 1988b: para. 5). Even in those schemes which have broadened the range of outcome measures (to include for example, social behaviour and post-compulsory schooling outcomes) and which have augmented these with some consideration of input and process indicators, there has until recently been an almost complete reliance on quantifiable data and a consequent undervaluing of qualitative indicators.

The climate does now seem to be changing, however, with key groups acknowledging that any framework 'would need to take adequate note both of quantitative and qualitative indicators' (CIPFA 1988: 3). The question arises quite acutely, therefore, as to how schools should select from the many thousands of possible indicators those that are appropriate to their own evaluation needs; how, that is, they are to shift from the static quantitative/qualitative dichotomy which has hitherto determined that selection towards a more dynamic and flexible framework of options.

In a document already referred to, the Society of Chief Inspectors and Advisers offers some useful suggestions as to how such a framework might be developed through the use of what it terms 'the achievement indicator matrix' (SCIA 1989). The matrix is constructed on two major dimensions with a third dimension as an additional refinement. The first of these serves to differentiate the proximity of the indicator from the core target being evaluated and distinguishes three degrees of proximity: direct indicators (which immediately reflect the target behaviour), indirect indicators (which occur in support of the activity under review without capturing the behaviour itself) and contextual indicators (which are circumstantial to the activity). Thus, for example, a school that is concerned with promoting independent learning among its pupils might look to evidence of self-study in the classroom as a direct indicator, to supportive statements in school policy documents as an indirect indicator and to parental commitment to such statements as a contextual indicator.

The second dimension differentiates the level of explanatory power of a particular indicator and distinguishes between high-, medium- and low-inference indicators. A school committed to providing a framework of positive relationships within its overall pastoral system might, for example, view the priority it gives to pastoral work on the timetable as a useful high-inference indicator, the incidence of bullying in and around the school as a medium-inference indicator and post-school offending levels as a low-inference indicator with very limited explanatory power as far as this particular area of achievement was concerned. That is not to say, of course, that post-school offending levels would always operate as a low-inference indicator. With regard to other achievement areas it could well be found to have very high explanatory power.

The point of the model, then, is that it helps schools to select those indicators that best suit their own purposes, given the constraints within which they operate. In general, of course, schools would be expected to aspire towards the top left-hand corner of the matrix (see Table 1.1); to try and ensure, that is, that their indicators are taken, as far as possible, at the point of service and that they have a high correlation with the area of achievement being evaluated. But that is not always possible. The direct, high-inference indicator may present insurmountable problems in terms of time allocation, resourcing and specialist expertise. It may also, if used in isolation, present a partial view that brackets out the less tidy, contextual features of school life. The matrix helps us focus upon the really useful indicators for the job in hand, while not losing sight of those which, although arguably less appropriate, might well disclose

Table 1.1 A selection of indicators relating to academic progress

	Direct indicators	*Indirect indicators*	*Contextual indicators*
High-inference	SATs GCSE (H)	School policies (P)	INSET provision (P)
Medium-inference	Pupil motivation (C)	Teacher turnover (P)	Parental support (P)
Low-inference	Teaching styles (C)	Pupil demeanour (C)	Post-school pupil destinations (H)

Note
H = historical (output)
C = current (process)
P = predictive (input)

Source: Adapted from SCIA 1989: 12.

valuable insights and be more immediately accessible to those carrying out the evaluation.

The third dimension describes the time relationship of the indicator to the particular achievement area under consideration. Again, three categories can be distinguished: historical indicators, which draw on evidence which is complete (output data); current indicators, which draw on evidence taken while the activity is in progress (process data); and predictive indicators, which draw on evidence that purports to assess the likelihood of a particular target behaviour being achieved (input data). On this dimension, a school concerned with maximizing academic progress would view weighted attainment data (for example, SATs) as an historical indicator; teaching styles as a current indicator; and staff INSET provision as a predictive indicator (see Table 1.1). Such a school would need to ensure that it did not become pushed into using only hard output data (historical) or rely too heavily on predictors (input data); which might be another good reason for viewing with some scepticism the drive towards an ideal set of direct, high-inference indicators. An appropriate mix of historical, current and predictive indicators is desirable.

The longer one considers the role of performance indicators within the evaluative process, the more difficult it is to hang on to the kinds of reassuring simplicities that have in the past so often dominated the debate. The intelligent choice is between neither qualitative and quantitative indicators, nor between input and output measures, but between those indicators that more nearly fit the purpose and those that, though valuable in different contexts, are inappropriate or simply impracticable. If evaluation is beginning to come of age, it is because at last some of the old dichotomies are now recognized as redundant and what once seemed battle lines have become blurred, contestable boundaries.

This is one reason why John Gray's (1990) announcement of the Sheffield University Performance Indicators constitutes a timely and witty intervention (see Table 1.2). For a start there are only three of them, relating to 'academic progress', 'pupil satisfaction' and 'pupil–teacher relationships'; second, they are couched in the form of open-ended questions to which the answer categories are realistically blurred at their statistical edges; and, third, they are eminently usable.

Neither the SCIA 'achievement indicator matrix' nor the three Sheffield University Performance Indicators scheme lays claim to

Table 1.2 The three Sheffield University Performance Indicators

---

Academic progress
What proportion of pupils have made above average levels of progress over the relevant time-period?

Pupil satisfaction
What proportion of pupils in the school are satisfied with the education they are receiving?

Pupil-teacher relationships
What proportion of pupils in the school have a good or 'vital' relationship with one or more teachers?

Answer categories for all three questions

All or most		Well under half
	About half	
Well over half		Few

Source: Gray 1990: 218.

finality; but each is nevertheless significant in that it attempts to thread a way through the current debate on performance indicators. In effect, each allows us to trace our footsteps back through the maze-like intricacies of much of the debate towards a clear acknowledgement that, as far as educational evaluation is concerned, the only evidence worth gathering is evidence that illuminates existing practice and, in so doing, helps us to improve upon that practice. It places at the centre of our concerns the professional judgement of teachers – in respect of both the kinds of evidence that might best be gathered and the kinds of decisions that such evidence might usefully inform – and thereby serves as a timely reminder that only through the exercise of that teacherly judgement can educational evaluation ever make a serious impact on the quality of learning within schools.

Summary

The context within which evaluation is currently operating is characterized by two distinguishing features. The first of these is the demand for public accountability of a wide range of professional activities and practices, including those of the teaching profession. Of course, within any democracy some form of accountability is necessary and desirable. In this instance, however, the mechanisms of accountability are closely associated with the second feature of the current context; namely, the emphasis on increased centralized control of the curriculum and of the wider organizational and administrative aspects of schooling. The assumption here is 'that accountability involves conformity to external prescription, thus leaving little room for the exercise of professional discretion' (Elliott *et al.* 1981: 15).

This appropriation of public accountability by central government has done more than anything else to shape educational evaluation over the last decade. The consequences have been a general blurring of the distinction between evaluation on the one hand and a particularly hard-edged version of accountability on the other. Evaluation, however, has not simply accommodated itself to changing circumstances; it has worked creatively within the newly defined parameters in such a way as to resolve some of its earlier tensions. In particular, the pressures under which it has had to operate have served to highlight the key role of teachers within the evaluation process and to clarify the intrinsic and long-term purpose of evaluative enquiry. What is now required, as a complement to this emergent paradigm, is a notion of accountability based on the assumption 'that one's actions flow from personal judgement and decision rather than external prescription' (Elliott *et al.* 1981: 19). It is to the question of purpose and impact, and to this alternative perspective on accountability, that we shall now turn.

– 2 –

Why Evaluate?

Evaluation should not be seen as a kind of sloppy research. It has its own scholarly standards which it shares with the research community at large: like research it aspires to be rigorous in its gathering of evidence, scrupulous in relating its analyses to that evidence and impartial in its reporting procedures. In other respects, however, evaluation can be seen to differ markedly from much of what passes for educational research. It is difficult, for example, to conceive of an evaluation programme which does not aim to make some kind of impact on the thinking and practice of teachers and on the effective organization of the school as a whole. While this is also true of much educational research, it is not universally so. In thinking about the purpose of evaluation we are necessarily thinking also about the kinds of impact that might reasonably be expected of it.

Three broad areas of impact can be distinguished in trying to move towards a clearer definition of the purpose of educational evaluation:

1 Creating a context of shared understanding within which schools can begin to realize the need for change.
2 Improving the quality of classroom practice and of the wider organizational structures of schooling.
3 Countering some of the simplistic expectations that are too often imposed upon educational institutions from the outside.

Before discussing these areas of impact, however, we shall explore in a little more detail the particular approach to evaluation which the book as a whole is attempting to articulate. The notion of 'collegiality' – of collaborative enquiry based on shared understanding and knowledge – provides a necessary basis for this exploration.

A collegial approach

Early approaches to educational evaluation tended to highlight teachers' commitment to self-reflection within the context of their own classroom practice. (See for example, Elliott 1978.) Indeed, even in those instances where a collaborative dimension had been implicit in the evaluation design, the main purpose of the exercise would seem to have been the increased understanding of the teacher, or co-teachers, concerned (Armstrong 1981). This emphasis on self-reflection undoubtedly contributed to an increased articulacy within the teaching profession regarding the educational values it espouses, together with a greater awareness of the ways in which these espoused values work their way through into action. What it did not do, however, was acknowledge the extent to which innovative and reflective teachers can become professionally isolated within their own institutions. Nor did it further the development of strategies for breaking down that isolation within and across schools. That key term – 'the teacher as researcher' – remained, in other words, sadly, though firmly, in the singular.

Later approaches have tried to address this problem by placing the emphasis on the institutional structures that sustain educational evaluation; by appealing, as Helen Simons puts it, to 'the notion of the reflective school where the aim is to focus on the school directly and to evaluate collectively how it may be changed' (1987: 237). This emphasis has in many cases helped to raise the level of participation and systematic course planning within schools and, as such, has avoided some of the pitfalls of those earlier approaches: see for example, Mitchell 1984. It has also, however, served to blur the earlier, very clear focus on education as being intrinsically worthwhile in itself and possessing its own inherent values. In becoming participative, evaluation has to some extent become institutionalized; and, insofar as it has become institutionalized, it has also become yet another way of endorsing the bureaucratic and managerial values that sustain schools as institutions; a way, that is, 'of viewing human relationships in which people inside are encouraged to see each other in terms of their institutional roles' (Rizvi and Kemmis 1987: 296).

The bureaucratic mode of thought cuts deep and is heavily value laden. It is primarily concerned with what Alisdair MacIntyre (1985) terms 'extrinsic goods', which in the case of contemporary schooling might be taken as cost effectiveness, value for money and measurement by result; concerns that are very different from what he sees as the 'intrinsic goods' of educational practice, such as the quality of learning, independent thought and truthfulness. It is important, therefore, that, in gaining its own niche within the institutional context of schooling, evaluation should be driven by educational values, as well as by the bureaucratic and managerial values of the settings within which it is located. It is important, that is, to develop a genuinely collegial approach to evaluation, which (while avoiding the naive individualism of earlier approaches) 'resists the corrupting power of institutions' (MacIntyre 1985: 194).

The quality of collaboration and participation that the notion of collegiality implies has been analysed by the social theorist Jürgen Habermas (1970) in his influential discussion of what he terms the 'ideal speech situation'. According to this analysis the conditions required to make any consensus reached in discourse rational and true are that there should be no external constraints preventing participants from assessing evidence and argument and that each participant should have an equal and open chance to offer reasons and rebuttals. 'In short,' as Wilfred Carr and Stephen Kemmis put it,

> the ideal speech situation requires a democratic form of public discussion which allows for an uncoerced flow of ideas and arguments and for participants to be free from any threat of domination, manipulation or control.
>
> (1986: 142)

It is important to bear in mind that we are talking here about an ideal form of communication and social organization and that the conditions sketched above are not to be found in any real speech situation. The significance of Habermas (and his notion of the 'ideal speech situation') is that he draws out the, as yet, unrealized ideal implicit in all speech; just as Alasdair MacIntyre, in his discussion of bureaucratic modes of operation, draws out the prevailing tendency towards dehumanization implicit in all institutions. What each says about a highly generalized, anticipated set of social relations allows us to gain a stronger critical purchase upon the actual relationships which we form and which, in turn, form us. In that sense, as Anthony Giddens remarks, the notion of 'the ideal speech situation provides a critical measure of the insufficiencies of currently existing forms of interaction and social institutions' (1985: 131).

Collegiality, therefore, particularly within the current context, should not be seen as a set of achieved organizational structures, but as a corporate urge towards a more democratic and open style of working; and educational evaluation, insofar as it aspires towards collegiality, should be seen as part of that shared responsibility for openness and enquiry. Given the tight accountability constraints discussed in the previous chapter, any such aspiration is likely to present a considerable challenge, not only to senior management team members but to all members of a school staff. For what a collegial approach to evaluation means in practice is that teachers should relate to one another first and foremost as colleagues, not as fixed points within a hierarchical structure; that they should work towards a definition of their own interests, rather than accept uncritically interests that are externally imposed upon schools; and that their prime concern should be the quality of learning of the young people they teach, rather than the bureaucratic vagaries of cost analysis and systems management.

Certain aspects of this approach approximate closely to the notion of 'democratic evaluation' advanced by Barry MacDonald (1976) in his early attempt to offer a political classification of evaluation studies. According to this classification a clear distinction can be made between three ideal types of evaluation: bureaucratic, autocratic and democratic. The latter, MacDonald argued, is based upon the value of an 'informed citizenry', with the evaluator acting 'as broker in exchanges of information between groups who want knowledge of each other'. Within democratic evaluation, therefore, the 'techniques of data-gathering and presentation must be accessible to non-specialist audiences' and must be such as to give 'informants . . . control over (the) use of the information they provide' (1976: 134).

A collegial approach to evaluation incorporates most, if not all, of MacDonald's points, but pushes them further by dissolving the sharp distinction that he makes between the person who conducts the evaluation and those who are being evaluated. The key point to which the collegial approach returns is that any effective evaluation of contemporary schooling must involve an element of self-evaluation, which in turn must involve the willing participation of the whole staff of a school. Without that active participation, the impact of any evaluation programme is likely to be severely limited. The approach to evaluation outlined in this book is grounded, there-fore, in the practical and theoretical concerns of classroom teachers and, as such, aspires to be both collaborative and reflexive. This, of course, directly affects the kinds of impact we might expect from it.

Shared understanding

Questions about the impact of evaluation are, typically, couched in the terms, 'Does evaluation make a difference?' (Alkin, Daillak and White 1979). Positive responses to that question tend to emphasize the role of evaluation in providing an information base for policy or action. According to this view, the impact of evaluation can be seen as a natural, linear development: a problem exists; information or understanding is lacking; evaluation provides the missing knowl-edge; a solution is reached. The relation between research and evaluation on the one hand, and policy and practice on the other, is thereby rendered relatively simple. The implicit image, as Carol Weiss and Michael Bucuvalas suggest, is 'decision maker as fresh stencil . . . research imprints its message, and the decision maker is expected to transfer it to the stack of blank pages awaiting his action' (1980: 15).

It would perhaps be unwise to abandon this view altogether, since (when the issues are uncomplicated and there is a clear consensus on values) evaluation can, arguably, have this kind of direct impact on both policy and practice. The only problem is that, within the field of education, the issues being addressed are seldom uncomplicated and the chance of starting from a clear consensus on values is extremely slim. This is particularly so in the case of a collegial approach to evaluation carried out within schools by teachers who have first-hand experience of the complexity of the contexts within which they work. They are unlikely, for example, to look to research to tell them whether or not they have a truancy problem. If they have such a problem they will know about it and will be looking to evaluation to help them understand why such a problem exists and how it might best be alleviated.

It is rare, then, for evaluation in schools to have the kind of direct and visible impact that it is so often expected to have. Educational evaluation may on occasion provide definitive answers; but, usually, only in response to questions which, from the inside, are likely to appear fairly simplistic. When, as it should, evaluation tackles the big issues, its impact is necessarily less immediate, less visible and less direct. It works on the way practitioners and policy makers understand the problem. It does not offer a ready made solution. The pertinent question, therefore, in thinking about the purpose of evaluation, would seem not to be 'Does evaluation make a difference?', but 'What kinds of difference might evaluation make?' Or, to shift the focus of that question slightly, 'What significant differences in the quality of teaching and learning can evaluation begin to illuminate?'

That shift is one of perspective, too. It requires that evaluation should be seen not as a linear sequence but as an interactive process: a complex set of interconnecting insights and shared understandings. Insofar as educational evaluation makes anything happen, it does so by helping practitioners stand back and understand what *is* happening and, equally important, what *might* happen. From this altered perspective evaluation can be said to exert its influence through the provision of a common language, by means of which individuals and groups can begin to articulate the options that are open to them and to square these options with their own perceptions of their current practice.

In their valuable study of the impact of research on policy and practice in education, John Nisbet and Patricia Broadfoot discuss some of the ways in which research can exert that kind of influence. 'Research', they argue, 'can *alert* policy makers to emerging trends. In its *challenging* function, research probes the weak parts of policy. However, the same testing procedures can also confirm policies and practice . . . and thus perform a *stabilising* function' (added emphasis, 1980: 22). These three functions provide a simple frame within which to locate the kinds of interactive mechanisms by which evaluation can begin to make an impact on the work of schools.

Alerting

School A is a coeducational, 11–16 comprehensive. A couple of years ago the head of science became interested in economic and industrial understanding as a theme within her own teaching. Having passed on this interest to other teachers within her department, she persuaded the headteacher to let her try and map the extent to which, and ways in which, this theme was being developed across the curriculum. Consequently, she sent to all staff within the school a brief questionnaire designed to ascertain how, if at all, they drew out economic and industrial issues within their own teaching.

As a result of the feedback she gained from this exercise, she was able to signal to the staff some gaps in the provision that was being offered in relation to this theme. Other than those working in her own department, only those involved in specialist courses within information technology and business studies seemed to show much awareness of how economic and industrial issues might relate to their own subject areas. She was thereby able to alert other teachers to the need for thinking critically about their own practice in the area of economic and industrial understanding and, in the case of one department, to prompt a number of in-service training events focusing on aspects of this theme.

The project also, however, highlighted the positive achievements within the relatively small business studies department, which within this particular school had tended to be seen as marginal to the major concerns of the curriculum. The small-scale information gathering exercise initiated by the head of science was able, therefore, to alert the staff to the cross-curricular potential of the business studies department and to the particular skills and expertise of those teaching within that department. As a result the two members of this department were able to extend their roles within the school and, on a number of occasions, offer advice and practical support to other departments attempting to open up their work in this way.

Challenging

Within school B – a coeducational, 11–16 comprehensive – members of an active and stable English department decided to review the validity of their own commitment to mixed ability teaching. For the last five years they had been working closely together in developing cooperative group work as a way of organizing classroom learning. They were still excited by the quality of interaction and the way in which the range of viewpoints within the group enriched individual pupils' written work. Recently, however, they had begun to question the extent to which their handling of cooperative group work realized their own aim of developing to the full their pupils' capacity to make independent judgements and to negotiate freely with one another.

As a result they agreed to institute a system of occasional paired teaching, whereby each member of the department was able to act as observer to another member over a half-term period. Each pair discussed the focus of the observational enquiry and worked out a provisional checklist of questions that might be addressed by the observer. One pair, for example, came up with the following list of questions:

1 To what extent do the pupils have control over the particular tasks that are set within the class?
2 What is the nature of the interventions made by the teacher in the course of the small-group work?
3 What kinds of responses do pupils make to suggestions put forward by the teacher?
4 How do pupils progress from one task to another and to what extent do they themselves influence these transitions?

It became apparent throughout the exercise that, if these questions were to be fully addressed, more detailed feedback was required from the pupils themselves. As a result they were invited to volunteer their own views, through individual and small-group interviews, on the purpose and value of the lessons in which they had taken part. From this exercise, the department found that, contrary to its declared aim, a number of pupils felt that their control over the tasks they were undertaking was extremely limited and that, in a small number of cases, they had very little understanding of how those tasks related to their own interests and aspirations. The exercise, in other words, challenged the teachers concerned to review the ways in which they set particular tasks and the kinds of interventions they made within the context of cooperative group work.

Stabilizing

Evaluation fulfilled a rather different function in School C where it was used to confirm earlier insights and thereby helped to support and sustain developments which had already been implemented. Three years earlier this rural primary school had undertaken a full policy review and had subsequently developed a strong policy statement on equal opportunities. This statement, which covered a wide range of curricular and organizational issues, had now been in existence for over two years. In that time there had been considerable staff turnover and, in particular, some key changes within the senior management team. In the light of these changes the staff felt it was important to ascertain whether the original policy commitment was still reflected in the current practice of the school.

All staff were invited, first, to comment upon the policy statement relating to equal opportunities and, second, to make a note of any lessons or events they had been involved in over the last year which seemed to them to highlight the school's continuing commitment within this area. Almost the entire staff responded to this request and, of these, the vast majority felt that the statement was clear, comprehensive and practical. The only reservations that were expressed were about the level of detail appropriate to a policy document rather than about the broad principles the document espoused. More than half the staff also submitted notes on lessons they had taught or events they had supervised which had a strong equal opportunities dimension. These were then circulated among the staff as a basis for further discussion, with some being written up in more detail for inclusion in the school's yearly broadsheet to parents.

This exercise had a positive, stabilizing effect on the school. It confirmed the staff in their commitment to equal opportunities, while at the same time revitalizing their discussions about the curricular implications of that commitment. It is important to bear in mind, when considering the relationship between evaluation and change, that evaluation can be useful in confirming and sustaining earlier developments as well as in prompting new initiatives and responses. Sometimes, in other words, the most important function that evaluation can fulfil is to apply a brake to further change, by highlighting existing achievements and confirming that, with regard to specific aspects of its work, a school is remaining broadly on course.

Affecting practice

The examples given above illustrate some of the ways in which evaluation can influence the context of ideas within which teachers operate. The purpose of evaluation can also, however, be rationalized in terms of its more direct impact on the practical and organizational aspects of schooling; provided, that is, that it builds upon the kinds of shared understanding outlined in the previous section. Schools are under constant pressure to short circuit the collegial processes by which evaluation can begin to make a long-term impact. It is important to emphasize, therefore, that even when evaluation has worked its way through into improved practice, that improvement may only be the tip of the iceberg in terms of its overall impact on the culture of the school.

It is also important to note that, while raw examination data often suggests striking differences between the 'worst' and 'best' schools in a particular LEA, recent research gives consistently low estimates of the extent to which schools contribute differentially to their own pupils' performance. (See for example, Nuttall *et al.* 1989; Smith and Tomlinson 1989; Gray, Jesson and Sime 1990.) Thus, although schools do undoubtedly make a difference, that difference only partially accounts for the discrepancies in examination results across schools. That point must be borne in mind when thinking about the impact of evaluation on educational practice, since it suggests that the kinds of improvement that we might be looking to evaluation to provide are subtle and therefore difficult to gauge.

The broad areas of educational activity within which evaluation can fairly claim to have this kind of direct influence upon the work of schools can be categorized very broadly as *teaching quality, policy making* and *pupil achievement*. Within these areas schools can, over time, target specific aspects of organization and practice so as to focus their evaluative activity more sharply. Indeed, without a clear focus of this kind, evaluation greatly reduces its chances of impacting upon practice in any significant way. The key questions that follow are intended, therefore, to suggest within each of the three areas some of the points at which evaluation can begin to have a direct influence on both the organizational and pedagogical aspects of schooling.

Teaching quality

'The question of how to improve the quality of teaching is', as Wilfred Carr points out, 'quite properly perceived to be at the heart of the contemporary educational debate' (1989: 1). Teachers are clearly in the hot seat as far as this particular debate is concerned. Their perceived values and attitudes, as manifest in their classroom practice and their general behaviour towards pupils, have a major influence on the learning that takes place within the school. In that respect, even under the terms of the statutory curriculum, the teaching profession retains considerable power.

As a starting point, therefore, it may be useful to distinguish some of the kinds of teacher behaviour that can be targeted when thinking about the impact of any evaluation exercise. These include:

- Task setting: are the tasks appropriate to the aims of the lesson and the abilities of the pupils? Are they clearly articulated? Do they relate to the requirements of the statutory curriculum?
- Pupil–teacher interaction: is the teacher's time fairly divided among the pupils? Do the interactions serve to focus and deepen the work? Are the teacher's interventions simply prompts and prods or do they also seek to be genuinely responsive?
- Questioning: do the teacher's questions lead pupils to think more clearly and express themselves more precisely? What kinds of response do cueing and testing questions receive? Which pupils respond to which kinds of questions?
- Content selection: how does this relate to the curriculum as a whole? Is it relevant to the needs of all the pupils within the particular teaching group? Are there any notable omissions in terms of the key cross-curricular concerns of the school curriculum?
- Recording and reporting: do the recording procedures take account of individual differences within the group? How are the teacher's records reported to pupils and parents? What contribution do pupils themselves make to recording their own progress and achievements?

These are, of course, only some of the categories that relate to the potential impact of evaluation on the quality of teaching within the classroom. One might well add to this list, for example, the broad category of off-site learning, which would include work experience, community service and the wide range of activities that pupils can undertake within the field of citizenship education. The precise focus, within any collegial approach to evaluation, will depend upon the school's particular priorities. The categories listed above do, however, provide an indication of the kinds of areas within which such an approach might have a discernible influence on the quality of teaching within a specific institution.

Policy making

School policy is another area within which evaluation can make a discernible impact. But there is an important general point that needs to be made regarding the relation between policy and practice. For me this point came across most clearly when studying the

various school and LEA policy statements on multicultural education and anti-racist teaching that were developed in the early 1980s
(Nixon 1985: 38–56). Put somewhat crudely, the point is that a
statement of policy can have little value unless it is part of a whole-
school developmental programme which reaches out into the community that the school serves. Policy is more than just the attainment
of a policy statement. It involves, also, an active involvement in
making policy work. This is true, I believe, within areas other than
multicultural education and is particularly pertinent to the current
context.

That general point has relevance for any evaluation study which
focuses upon the broad area of policy making. Schools might, therefore, begin to take their bearings within that area by considering the
following kinds of questions:

- Staff involvement: are the staff fully involved in the development
  of policy? What are the mechanisms for mediating between that
  involvement and the production of a final policy statement? Do
  those mechanisms work?
- Implementation: are existing policies being implemented? If
  so, how? If not, why not? What steps are being taken to ensure
  that policy statements currently being formulated will be fully
  implemented?
- Implications: what implications do particular policies have for
  different subject specialisms? What are their implications for
  senior management? Have these implications been taken on
  board?
- Dissemination: are the school policies known about and understood by the staff as a whole and by pupils and governors? What
  consultation procedures are in place? Are these procedures
  adequate and effective?
- Policy review: do the existing policy statements meet the current
  needs and concerns of the school? How often and by what means
  are they reviewed? Does the timing of the policy review take
  account of the turnover rate among staff?

A serious consideration of these and similar features of the policy
making process, together with the kinds of questions that they
generate, would enable evaluation to make a fairly direct and pertinent impact on that process. This is an important contribution that
evaluation can make, though in itself it does not produce the evidence by which schools can begin to judge the extent to which their

policies are working their way through into practice. In order to generate that kind of evidence, evaluation needs to look to other outcomes. The most important of these relates to the overall achievement of pupils.

Pupil achievement

This is by far the most difficult area to think about in terms of the direct impact of evaluation, partly because it is dependent upon the other two categories, and partly because it so easily collapses into a reductionist debate about examination results. That debate can be important, when it sensitively and skilfully attempts to problematize the notion of school effectiveness. But my own feeling is that it remains light years away from offering any informed view of what the curriculum in action is all about. That kind of perspective can only be gained by looking at a much broader range of pupil achievement, within and outside the classroom, and by taking into account process as well as outcome measures. The question remains, therefore, as to how evaluation can gain a direct purchase on those aspects of pupil achievement that are not catered for by the public examination system or by the systematic testing procedures introduced under the umbrella of the statutory curriculum.

Any response to that question needs to take account of the following, often unrecognized, aspects of pupil achievement. These are even more provisional, arguable and open to wider interpretation than the previous questions. For that very reason they ought, within any collegial approach to evaluation, to be considered as a major area of impact.

- Pupil interaction: who interacts with whom in the classroom? Are particular pupils excluded from the general pattern of interaction? What is the quality of interaction?
- Self-directed learning: do the pupils understand the rationale of the tasks they are undertaking? To what extent do they have control over the development of those tasks? Do the pupils ever set their own tasks and, if so, under what circumstances?
- Off-site learning: what kinds of learning take place outside the classroom? How are these off-site – and sometimes extra-curricular – achievements recorded? Do they feed back into on-site learning? If so, how?
- Pupil self-assessment: how do teachers, and pupils, conceive of

the idea of pupil self-assessment? Is it built into the programmes of work offered across the full range of subjects? How is it organized?

- Recording and reporting: how are pupils' achievements reported back to the parents and pupils concerned? Do the records distinguish between individual and group achievements? Do they invite a response?

Informing, explaining, persuading

Andy Hargreaves's concern that 'hope, faith and optimism have not so much permeated the discussions and evaluation of SCI [school-centred innovation] as consumed them' (1989: 19) is a pertinent reminder of the need for schools to evaluate these crucial aspects of their own practice. It is also, however, a reminder of the need to engage in critical dialogue with a wide range of constituencies – parents, governors, researchers and policy makers – and, moreover, to base that dialogue on something other than good intentions. Evaluation can thus be seen to have a third sphere of influence: beyond its indirect impact upon teachers' understanding of their own practice and its more direct impact on teaching and learning, it can also – sometimes – fulfil a communicative function beyond the immediate community of staff and pupils.

Schools have a potentially vital role to play in countering the simplicities that are so often peddled as informed educational commentary: falling standards, low teacher morale, lack of discipline and the like. These may be myths. Even so, they are powerful myths and require the kind of rejoinder that only research-based evaluation – with its emphasis on processes as well as outcomes, analyses rather than taken for granted assumptions – can provide. Seen in this light, critical insider accounts of work undertaken in schools can help to highlight the complexities of schooling and thereby serve to inform, explain and, if necessary, persuade others of the likely implications of those complexities.

Take, for example, the following brief extract from a detailed study, carried out by a nursery school teacher in America, focusing on the ways in which her group of four- and five-year-olds developed their writing skills:

One day, John . . . asked me, 'Why do all my words have *a* in them. Why?' When I talked about words having lots of *a*'s and

e's in them he asked, 'Why is the *a* always the second letter of
all my words?' He then said, 'I never have any *h's* in my words.
Are there any words that start with *h*?' I told him some. He
then asked, 'But how about in the middle of the word?' I
thought and thought and came up with Ohio. He seemed
pleased and satisfied. I think this conversation tells a lot about
the value of giving a young child like John the freedom to
experiment with his own language and how he hears its
sounds. He was doing some deep thinking for a five year old.

(Awbrey 1989: 58)

Clearly the teacher is here recording an insight which has important implications for the way in which she approaches the teaching
of writing within her own classroom. Her study also, however, has
important things to say to other key groups: teachers working in
different contexts and with different age groups, parents, those with
responsibility for implementing the curriculum as a whole and
(thinking of the British context) school governors who urgently
require this kind of insight into how the curriculum works in practice. This single instance is an eloquent testimony to the pedagogical
complexity that lies, often unacknowledged, behind the current
terminology of 'attainment targets' and 'profiles of study' and to the
way in which teachers can enable the wider educational community
to understand the implications of that complexity.

We are talking here, of course, about a particular kind of impact
that must be seen as the outcome of a long and sometimes difficult
process. The journey from shared understanding, through improved
practice, to some kind of public and authoritative statement – that
informs, explains and persuades – involves a long-term commitment by the staff as a whole. The conditions necessary for teachers
to be able to enter into professional dialogue with other groups
through the process of evaluation cannot be achieved overnight. But
if teachers are to attain to a notion of professionalism that relies
upon something other than their own assertion of autonomy – if, in
other words, they are to respond to the challenge of increased
accountability without being defeated by its cruder manifestations –
they must travel along this road.

The journey has a great deal to do with teachers' growing regard
for what Hargreaves refers to as 'the importance of the active,
interpreting self in social interaction'. In this view, teachers are 'not
just bundles of skill, competence and technique; they are creators

of meaning, interpreters of the world and all it asks of them' (1989: 76). It is important, therefore, that the impact of evaluation should not be thought of in purely mechanistic terms: as, for example, the acquisition and monitoring of new teaching techniques or subject expertise. To treat these in isolation is to adopt a damagingly deficit view of the role of the teacher. Only when that role is viewed critically in relation to the broader issues of professional status and recognition can evaluation begin to have a serious impact on policy matters and so influence not only the wider debate on schooling, but ultimately the basic conditions of teachers' work.

Summary

This chapter has emphasized that evaluation is a process and that the long-term nature of that process must be understood if it is to have any real impact on teaching and learning and on the way in which these are perceived within the wider community. In particular it has emphasized that the prime purpose of evaluation is the creation of a context of ideas within which critical self-reflection is seen as a prerequisite both of improved practice and of genuine accountability: evaluation, at best, sails to its goal by a side wind. In tracing through the implications of this argument, the following chapter now shifts towards the more practical concerns of planning and implementation.

– 3 –

A Formative Process

'Yes, we know evaluation is important, but how do we get started? And once we've got started how do we keep going?' This is a fairly common response from teachers to people like myself who argue that evaluation is not just an optional extra but a prerequisite of teacher professionalism. It is usually accompanied by equally pertinent comments regarding conditions of work, time constraints, and received notions of the teacher's role as being necessarily action oriented: 'How can we possibly carve out the necessary space for evaluation? How can we find the time? How can we be both reflective and proactive?'

These are important questions and highlight the extent to which much of the literature on institutional self-evaluation has all too often been either exhortatory or crudely programmatic. In this chapter I shall try to take these questions seriously and show how schools can relate the more reflective concerns of the evaluation process to the specific staff development needs of teachers and to the more general requirements of whole-school curriculum reform. In so doing I shall be highlighting the importance of careful planning, which is both purposeful in its specification of likely outcomes and unrushed in its achievement of consensus regarding the form and focus of the evaluation.

Thinking ahead

Since evaluation has developed historically within the broad context of applied, empirical research, it is often seen as falling naturally into certain familiar phases:

- planning, setting up and focusing;
- gathering evidence;
- analysis and dissemination; and
- utilization.

A wide range of evaluative practice – from in school, through local LEA evaluations to regional and national studies – is rationalized in terms of some such phased progression (see for example, Hopkins 1989: 38). Indeed, the argument and structure of this book are couched within a set of assumptions which are closely aligned to this notion of evaluation as a form of rational and empirically based enquiry that relies upon some such phasing. That notion does, however, raise a number of problems which need addressing if schools are to relate it to their own particular circumstances and agendas.

The central problem is that as soon as we begin to reduce a complex process into sequential categories we run the risk of rendering it mechanical. The whole point of intellectual enquiry is that it is heuristic; which is to say that, at the outset, we cannot know what, in the end, we shall have learnt. Indeed, if we could, we would be beyond the need for enquiry anyway. It is essential, therefore, to see the process of evaluation as all of a piece and, while drawing on the idea of phased progression, not to be too rigidly constrained by it. In practice, the phases are rarely discrete and may be seen, in retrospect, to bear little relation to the complexity of the process they are supposed to denote.

The tendency to compartmentalize, and thereby reduce, that process is frequently reinforced by the terminology used to describe it. It is fairly common now, for example, to force a distinction between evaluation, on the one hand, and monitoring and review on the other. Much of the evaluation literature emanating from TVEI and TRIST has added to this confusion by collapsing the notion of in-school evaluation into one or other of its constituent elements. (See for example, Eraut, Pennycuick and Radnor undated: 12; Holly, James and Young 1987: 44.) What should be seen a single, continuous process is thereby needlessly carved up into a number of separate and discrete activities.

This inevitably leads to an unhelpful divorce between evidence and analysis, with the frequent result that too much time is given to data gathering and too little time to thinking about what kind of evidence is required and to processing and sifting the evidence as it is being gathered: the classic problem of data overload. It is important to remember, therefore, that in research terms a little evidence goes a long way. What is important is not the amount of evidence gathered, but its relevance to the focus of the enquiry and the extent to which it is worked and reworked so as to generate fresh insights and question existing assumptions.

Wynne Harlen and John Elliott have produced a useful checklist for planning an evaluation which is worth quoting in full because of the important emphasis it places upon the need to foreshadow, during the planning stage, the various methodological and substantive issues that are likely to arise in any evaluation:

1 Reasons, purposes and motivations
   - who wants the evaluation to be carried out?
   - what reasons do they have for wanting the evaluation to be done?
   - who wants the information it will provide?
   - what reasons do they have for wanting the information?
   - who else should have the information?
2 Worthwhileness
   - what possible actions or decisions can be taken as a result of the evaluation?
   - what possible actions or decisions have been pre-empted?
   - what constraints are there on the planning and execution of the evaluation?
3 Interpretation of the evaluation task
   - what views do those involved hold about the nature of the evaluation?
   - what is the existing decision-making system and how does the evaluation relate to it?
4 Subjects of the evaluation
   - what will be evaluated?
   - what kinds of information are required?
5 The evaluators
   - who will gather the information?
   - what kinds of information are required?
6 Evaluation methods

- are the methods to be used appropriate to the information required?
- can the methods be devised, if necessary, and applied in the time available?
- what resources, equipment, back-up facilities are required for the methods to be used?
- will the methods for data collection be acceptable to those who will be involved in supplying information?

7 Time schedule
- what time is available for the evaluation?
- can the information required be gathered and processed in that time?

8 Control of information
- what procedures, if any, will govern the collection and release of information?
- how will ownership of the information be decided?

9 Criteria for making judgements or decisions
- who will decide the criteria to be applied in using the information?
- will there be the need or possibility for applying alternative criteria?

10 Reporting
- in what form will the evaluation be reported?
- will those involved be shown the report before it is made final?
- who will be the designated audience of the report?
- what steps will be taken to see that the report reaches the designated audience?

(Harlen and Elliott 1982: 296–8)

Some of these questions are more relevant than others. The checklist was, after all, designed for use in a wide variety of contexts. Nevertheless, this remains a useful starting point for any school attempting to think through the kinds of issues that have to be addressed in the course of any evaluation. In particular it raises important questions about roles and responsibilities, about the agreement upon a common focus and task, and about the ethics of evaluation. If evaluation is to be a genuinely formative process, in the sense of feeding back into the practical and organizational structures of schooling, these issues must be addressed at the outset.

Taking responsibility

The question of who will carry out the evaluation is a crucial one and, as Harlen and Elliott suggest (see 5 above), is closely related to the question of what kinds of evidence are to be gathered. Since, however, we are here concerned with the evaluation of the whole curriculum, it is essential that some mechanism is found to ensure that its purposes are fully accepted and understood by each member of staff. In relatively small schools this may not present a great problem, but in larger schools considerable attention needs to be given to the kind of organizational framework within which a collegial approach to evaluation might best be developed. In effect this will almost certainly mean that some staff forum in which issues relating to evaluation can be talked through and translated into a whole-school strategy will need to be identified or created. Some initial and crucial decisions have to be made, therefore, concerning the constitution of that forum and its relation to the main policy making bodies within the institution.

It may be, of course, that within the existing framework there is already a forum that might usefully absorb in-school evaluation into its brief. But this is unlikely. Most policy making bodies are plagued by overcrowded agendas. To pile new responsibilities on to existing working groups may mean that other items are crowded out or that evaluation, if it gets a look in at all, is simply seen as a way of ratifying earlier policy decisions and initiatives. Either way, this is likely to cause tensions and reduce evaluation to a fairly marginal activity. Existing working groups will no doubt want to concern themselves with evaluation within their own terms of reference but, in addition, some more specialist group may well be needed to coordinate the overall evaluation strategy and ensure that it relates to the concerns of the school as a whole.

The setting up of such a group should not be seen, however, as an attempt to mark out a territory with fixed boundaries. Evaluation relates to *every* aspect of school life and to the work of *all* teachers. Any suggestion that this area of activity is a closed system will not only be counterproductive, but will be contrary to the collegial spirit that informs effective in-school evaluation. The reasons for devolving overall responsibility to a specific group are purely practical. They should not be confused with the purpose of the exercise itself, which is centrally concerned with the idea of teachers taking responsibility for their own professional lives and of schools taking responsibility for their own professional practices.

This brings us to the crucial question of how such a group should be constituted. If evaluation is to be seen as a genuinely participative activity, its planning and oversight cannot be seen simply as a function of the senior management team; particularly so, since it is essential to distance it from any association with managerial appraisal. The constitution of the group will need to be thought through in terms of the existing management structure of the school, its general ethos and its capacity for self-criticism. Each of these factors, needless to say, is problematic. As a general rule, it is useful to keep the size of a coordinating group of this kind as small as possible, while ensuring that the various interests within the school are fairly represented.

The following list of questions (adapted from Nixon 1989c) highlights some of the decisions that will need to be made in constituting such a group.

- Should a member, or members, of the senior management team have automatic membership of the evaluation coordinating group?
- Should the members of the group be assigned or elected? If the former, by whom?
- If the latter, should this be on the basis of an open election for which all staff are eligible to stand?
- Regardless of whether members are to be assigned or elected, should they be drawn from specified constituencies within the community of the school?
- How should the chairing of the group be determined?
- Should provision be made for the cooption of members (1) from within the school; and (2) from non-teaching staff?
- If the principle of cooption is to be adopted, what individuals and groups from outside the school might have useful experience and expertise to draw on?
- For what length of time should individuals serve as members of the coordinating group?

Whatever its constitution a coordinating group of this kind needs to report on a regular basis to the full staff meeting, so that the staff as a whole can be informed and consulted about the evaluation as it is being planned and formulated. There needs, therefore, to be a mechanism for referring recommendations to the full staff. The relation between the coordinating group and other policy making bodies and working parties within the school also needs to be clearly defined. Given the variety of organizational structures within different schools, it is not possible (even if it were desirable) to abstract a single system that would cover all cases. It is important to emphasize, however, that what needs to be established is not a linear chain of command, but a complex process of consultation that involves the coordinating group in liaising with a variety of other groups and individuals at different points within the organizational structure of the school.

As such, the coordinating group should not be seen as solely responsible for carrying out the evaluation. On the contrary, it is their responsibility to ensure that, as far as possible, evaluation becomes a whole-school concern to which as many colleagues as possible relate in terms of reflecting upon their own and each other's practice. The purpose of the group is to ensure a common focus, to act as a key reference point for individuals and collaborative teams who are attempting to evaluate their own work, and to ensure that insights and information are fed back to the staff as a whole and, where appropriate, to governors, parents and other interested parties. Theirs is, in short, essentially a coordinating and facilitating role.

This emphasis on establishing at the outset an organizational framework may seem somewhat managerial in tone. It must be emphasized, however, that what we are aiming at is not a piecemeal approach to evaluation which relies upon a few enthusiasts, but a collegial approach for which the staff as a whole assume responsibility. Such an approach cannot be left to chance. If it is to prove effective, in-school evaluation requires a clearly defined structure within which to operate and develop. Without some such structure, any attempt at evaluation is likely to be short lived and limited in its overall impact.

Progressive focusing

Structures, of course, do not just happen: they have to be constructed and, having been constructed, they have to be worked at. This is a particularly important point to bear in mind when considering the question of focus. All too often focusing is simply seen as a preliminary, one-off activity. According to this view, the focus of the evaluation, once agreed, remains conveniently static. In practice, however, the initial focus almost always has to be modified and refined in the light of new evidence. The process of negotiating and renegotiating a focus is necessarily a protracted one and the structure within which those negotiations take place must, therefore, be flexible and resilient.

An important first step in beginning to clarify the focus of the evaluation is to review any existing evidence that may be relevant. This may include documents produced within the school but will also, almost certainly, include relevant LEA documents as well as articles and research reports in professional journals: a daunting task, maybe, but one which becomes less so when the combined expertise of the staff is drawn on. Let us say, for example, that the agreed focus has been initially defined in terms of gender issues relating to option choices at 14 + . A review of the relevant literature can help to clarify what precisely those issues might be and to generate some specific questions that need addressing. Moreover, a number of staff, as well as LEA advisers and personnel in local institutions of higher education, may be able to point to key readings that can help in clarifying the initial focus in this way, thereby establishing early on a broad base of involvement in the evaluation.

An important point underpins this emphasis on the need to draw on as wide a range of reference as possible before clarifying the focus of the evaluation. A common mistake in applied research generally, and research-based evaluation in particular, is to rush into gathering evidence before the nature of the problem is clearly framed. Much time is thereby wasted in gathering either too much evidence or evidence which, in retrospect, proves to be inappropriate. Some such wastage is inevitable. But it can, with a little circumspection, be kept to a minimum. The general point to be stressed is that the kinds of evidence collected should depend upon the nature of the problem being addressed, not the other way round.

In this respect evaluation differs markedly from some kinds of ethnographic research and also from the kind of naturalistic description associated with fictional art forms. The intrinsic value of the case study (where it is something other than a mere exemplar) and the novel (where it is something other than a mere pot boiler) lies in the material upon which each is based. Evaluation, while seeking to avoid the cruder excesses of instrumentalism, has of necessity to be more streamlined. It has to keep pulling back and reassuring itself that the material upon which it is working is relevant to the needs of the institution and the individuals upon which it relies. It cannot afford too much wastage. It has to keep coming back, through negotiation and renegotiation, to the problem as understood by the constituencies to which it is ultimately answerable.

This suggests a rather different process of phased progression than that usually presented in step by step manuals on in-school evaluation. We are talking, in other words, about a cyclical process involving successive rounds of brief, condensed data gathering interspersed by clearly bounded periods that connect into an extended analysis of the issues being addressed. What evidence one collects, and how one collects it, is never simply a technical matter. It is always deeply methodological and, as such, involves a consideration of why the particular evidence one is drawing on is both pertinent and relevant; and, equally, if not more importantly, whether the questions one is asking of it are worth asking.

We can begin to rationalize the evaluation process, then, in terms of two interwoven threads: the evidence and the construction put upon that evidence. It is the spinning of those threads, and their interweaving, that constitutes the peculiar satisfaction to be derived from designing an effective evaluation programme. No one programme, if sensitive to the context within which it is to be applied, can be identical to another. No blueprint, unfortunately or otherwise, is available. While learning to live with contingency, we can, nevertheless, draw some lessons from the way in which, when effectively spun, those threads combine to good effect.

These lessons, drawn from my own experience of evaluation in a wide variety of contexts, can be summarized as follows:

- The build up to the evaluation should be careful, meticulous and unrushed and should include a full review of the literature available, and involve the whole staff.
- The periods of data collection should be conducted over clearly defined periods of time and should be condensed and intensive.
- Following each data-collection period, there should be an opportunity to refine and sharpen the focus of the evaluation and to reformulate the questions being addressed.

So what does this look like in practice? For convenience, let us take a twelve-month time span. The first quarter would be spent preparing the groundwork for the evaluation: negotiating an initial focus, reviewing the available literature and deciding on the kinds of evidence to be gathered during the first period of data collection. The second quarter would involve a two- to three-week period of data collection followed by a preliminary sifting of the evidence gathered; a clarification of the key issues being addressed; and a decision as to the kinds of evidence required to explore these issues further. During the third quarter further evidence would be gathered, again during a two- to three-week period, followed by a more detailed analysis of the key issues. The final quarter might then be spent gathering any further evidence that seemed necessary and returning to any external sources of information to deepen and contextualize the insights that were emerging.

This hypothetical design does not, of course, take account of school terms (although a quarterly system that involves periods of consecutive fieldwork and analysis may in fact be well suited to a three-term calendar). Nor does it allow an opportunity for retrospective analysis and summative reporting. It does, however, suggest the kind of balance that ought to be achieved between time spent on data gathering and time spent on preparation and on going analysis. In doing so it challenges the popular misconception that as an evaluator one somehow collects one's evidence in the dark and then analyses that evidence in the light of a prespecified focus. In practice, clarity of focus is as much an outcome, as a prespecification, of evaluation.

This emphasis on progressive focusing has some relevance to our earlier discussion of performance indicators. It may well be, of course, that the current concern with performance indicators is a passing phase: a key element within the present context of increased accountability and centralized control but, nevertheless, transient in its impact. Insofar as schools, for whatever reason, view performance indicators as fundamental to their evaluation concerns, they should, therefore, see them not as pre-ordained benchmarks, but as markers that require careful and judicious selection. Evaluation cannot be reduced to a naive testing device. It is the means by which schools can begin to sift and understand the criteria by which they and others might most effectively judge the value of their own practice. Evaluation depends, in other words, not upon a prior selection from a range of externally imposed performance indicators, but upon the willingness of teachers to articulate, through a process of analysis based on evidence, those indicators that they themselves find to be of critical value.

Much is made, in the available evaluation literature, of the need to select appropriate methods of data gathering. This is, of course, a necessary element in the preparation of any evaluation, but methods are not so many jars on a shelf to be reached down in accordance with a well-tried recipe. Methods define themselves in terms of the questions being addressed and those questions, as we have seen, have to be defined over time. The tastiest recipes, as far as evaluation is concerned, are invariably discovered rather than received. So the methods, too, have to evolve and adapt.

This means that a variety of data sources may be drawn on even within a relatively small-scale evaluation programme. The methodological variety that this gives rise to is often graced with the name 'triangulation', and is advanced as a general precept for ensuring that evidence drawn from one source is checked against other sources of evidence. We shall return to the notion of methodological triangulation when we consider, by way of conclusion to Chapter 6, the problem of building a composite picture of the curriculum in action. It is an important notion, but one which should be seen not as a rule to be slavishly adhered to but as a natural consequence of pursuing evaluation as a creative discipline.

Procedural principles

So far, this account makes no mention of the key ethical issues which need to be thought through at the outset if difficulties are to be avoided later. These issues roughly cover the last three points specified by Harlen and Elliott (i.e. control, criteria and reporting) but for the purposes of the present argument might best be seen as relating to the problems of:

- gaining access to the main sources of evidence;
- releasing that evidence internally once it has been gathered;
- negotiating its release more widely if this is deemed appropriate;
- ensuring some measure of balance in any report issuing from the evaluation.

Gaining access

As far as access is concerned, the point that needs to be stressed is that this should be negotiated, not assumed. Moreover, those allowing access (for example, to their classrooms, to the written work produced within those classrooms and to their own professional records) should understand the nature and purpose of the undertaking. This may, of course, involve some communication with parents and pupils as well as colleagues. Building into the evaluation process these kind of preparatory procedures is necessarily time consuming and is another reason, therefore, why the run up to the evaluation should be careful, meticulous and unrushed.

If this principle of negotiated access is neglected, the evaluation may well serve to alienate sections of the school community. Evaluation, when handled badly, can be deeply disruptive. It is important, therefore, to get it right and getting it right means taking the need for initial consultation seriously. A coordinating group convinced of the importance of evaluation can all too easily assume that others share their enthusiasm and that those who do not can be bulldozed into change. The history of curriculum development over the last decade reveals the wrong-headedness of this approach. Unless those responsible for coordinating the evaluation have the patience to take the whole staff along with them, a collegial approach to evaluation has no chance. Collegiality means, among other things, keeping faith with the faithless.

Internal release

Issues relating to the release of evidence are often discussed somewhat narrowly in terms of the twin principles of confidentiality and anonymity. As far as the internal release of evaluation evidence is concerned, the reliance on these principles is, I would argue, unrealistic and misguided. Even within fairly large schools individuals are easily identifiable by their colleagues in terms of the posts they hold, the responsibilities they assume and the principles they espouse. Procedures organized around the need for confidentiality and anonymity are likely, therefore, to be of little other than ritualistic value, while systems of internal reporting based on those procedures turn all too often into a guessing game whereby the readership is more concerned with working out who did and said what than with addressing the major issues arising.

It is difficult, moreover, to see how, if a strict rule of confidentiality is applied, a genuinely collegial approach to in-school evaluation can be developed. Such an approach, while not trampling too heavily upon the secret gardens of the curriculum, must open doors on to those hidden aspects of curriculum practice and let the light in. Ultimately, that means building confidence, not breaking it. But it also, I believe, means breaking with a particular notion of confidentiality that can serve to reinforce divisions and stratifications. A more appropriate principle to govern the internal release of evidence, therefore, would be one whereby a school, in assuming responsibility for its own evaluation, would 'treat all relevant interviews, meetings, oral and written exchanges with participants . . . as on the record, unless specifically asked to treat them as confidential' (PRAISE 1987: 292). That way all those involved know where they are.

Negotiated release

Where evaluation evidence is to be released more widely further negotiation will be necessary. It cannot be assumed, for example, that a report produced for internal consumption is thereby appropriate for a more general audience of parents, governors, teachers in other schools, LEA advisers, etc. Some system of negotiated release therefore needs to be instituted, whereby the release of evidence is renegotiated in terms of different readerships. This calls, at the outset, for a very clear specification of audience and, throughout, for a willingness to redraft evaluation statements and reports as the findings are made increasingly public.

Such a system, it should be noted, flies in the face of received wisdom regarding the ethics of educational evaluation. According to the prevailing orthodoxy, the principles of confidentiality and anonymity must be carefully adhered to, at the outset, in order to protect participants at the final point of release. My argument is that, within a collegial approach to evaluation, those principles are inappropriate and that participants can be adequately protected through a system of negotiated release whereby confidentiality can be conferred, retrospectively, by producing a more generalized account (or possibly more than one account) for outside audiences.

Contested impartiality

Expecting evaluation to achieve conclusive impartiality is to misunderstand its distinctive quality. Since, as Ernest House (1980: 72) points it, 'logical certainty is achievable only within a closed, totally defined system like a game', evaluative judgements ought not to be seen as a version of umpiring whereby decisions are made within a fixed frame of reference which renders them instantaneously authoritative. For a start, no such frame exists and, second, there is always the possibility of new evidence coming to light which will render the old judgements inadequate or simply wrong.

This does not mean that impartiality ought not to be a goal towards which evaluation aspires, but that its achievement should always be seen as provisional. There is no permanent, fixed point from which the evaluator can adopt a genuinely once and for all, neutral perspective.

Evaluation reports should, therefore, be speculative, opening up questions and issues for further consideration, rather than offering final and definitive accounts. Any claim to impartiality must, in other words, include the opportunity for the grounds upon which that claim is made to be contested. In practice this means that the reporting procedures should be such as to allow for divergent views and informed responses to be incorporated into the evaluation. An evaluation report is but a single, albeit integral, voice within a complex deliberative and reflective process of whole-school, and often cross-school, consultation.

Any coordinating group will need to consider these arguments very carefully, however, and would do well to refer to the literature that takes a different, sometimes more positivist, line from my own. The value, I believe, of the line suggested here is that it comes clean about the extent to which teachers expose their own assumptions and practices in adopting a collegial approach to evaluation; that it sees the release of evidence not as a single event, but as a continuing process that requires periodic renegotiation; that it acknowledges the differing needs of, and problems posed by, the various external audiences to which in-school evaluation may be addressed; and that it recognizes the inevitable provisionality of the knowledge derived from evaluation.

The political problems raised by the release of evaluation evidence within the current context of accountability and centralized control cannot be resolved by recourse to a particular set of in-house ethical principles; particularly so when these are framed within a legal–rationalistic overview that fails to acknowledge the contingency – sometimes, even, the sheer messiness – of everyday life in schools. A collegial approach to in-school evaluation means opening up, but opening up on one's own terms and at one's own pace. Insofar as general principles apply in these circumstances, they do so, I believe, in terms of a more expansive notion of collegiality than that suggested in much of the literature on the ethics of educational evaluation, with its heavy emphasis on the right to privacy and the rule of confidentiality. (See Pring 1987 and Simons 1989 for differing perspectives on this debate.)

Summary

Throughout this chapter I have tried to distance what I have termed the collegial approach to evaluation from a linear, rationalist model of curriculum research and development. Increasingly, that model seems to be based less on 'an interesting assumption reaching back to the Enlightenment' (House 1980: 64) than on a kind of magic: if you follow the necessary rituals in the pre-specified order you will arrive at 'the Truth'. There are, I have suggested by implication, at best only 'truths' and these direct us towards a coherence of viewpoint rather than towards any final correspondence between fact and definitive judgement: the truths to which evaluation can aspire are governed, that is, not by necessity but by contingency (Rorty 1989: 52.) At any point within the evaluation process one has to be thinking ahead, taking stock, looking back, glancing sideways . . . The process of preparation is in large part a matter of creating a social context that is sufficiently flexible, trusting and lasting to cope with the demands of this kind of formative enquiry.

The following three chapters outline some of the methods that can be used to gain a greater understanding of how the curriculum operates within specific institutional contexts. Taking as a starting point the notion of 'the whole curriculum', successive chapters focus on the need to gather evidence of the processes of teaching and learning within particular classrooms, on the interpretation of some easily accessible numerical data, and on the forms and uses of the research interview. These chapters are complementary in the sense that (as argued earlier) both process and outcome measures are essential for a full understanding of the curriculum in use. They are also framed by a tentative but continuing argument about the nature of the statutory curriculum. In the following chapter, therefore, I shall consider in some detail how the National Curriculum affects our understanding of 'the whole curriculum' and what the implications of this impact are for those committed to an evaluative stance towards their own, and their colleagues', practice.

– 4 –

The Whole Curriculum

It is often very difficult for teachers working alone in their classrooms to see the curriculum as all of a piece. The individual teacher can see her or his bit of it, of course, and may have a fairly keen sense of how that bit relates to some of the other bits. But the way in which schools are organized may well mean that, as far as most teachers and learners are concerned, the bits never add up. Or, if they do, only on paper, as boxes on a timetable or words in a curriculum policy. The National Curriculum – with its countless attainment targets and its heavy emphasis on discrete subject specialisms – has done little, if anything, to resolve this problem. The whole curriculum remains as elusive as ever.

The statutory curriculum

There is something odd about the idea of the whole curriculum. It suggests, after all, that there may be some other idea of the curriculum as either intrinsically fragmented or necessarily partial; a curriculum, that is, which is not, and does not aspire to be, all of a piece. Yet if a curriculum lacks such aspirations, it is arguable whether it can be properly described as a curriculum at all, any more than a random collection of verses can be described as a poem or a syllogism be derived from a single proposition. The notion of the whole curriculum is perhaps, therefore, a necessary rhetorical device only when the very idea of curriculum coherence is at risk.

This helps to explain why, within the present context, the NCC has recently chosen to emphasize that notion. As David Hargreaves (1990) has pointed out,

> One of the best ideas that HMI contributed to the [curriculum] debate was the principle that the curriculum should be broad, balanced and coherent. The DES adopted the notion of breadth and balance, but somehow and for unknown reasons the concept of coherence was quietly dropped.

Extending that argument, one might add that the NCC would now seem to have quietly picked it up again and, if not exactly running with it, is at least ensuring that, through the work of its Whole Curriculum Committee, the concept of coherence receives some recognition.

It is through this committee that *Curriculum Guidance 3: The Whole Curriculum* (NCC 1990a) has been issued. This key document distinguishes what it calls the 'cross-curricular elements' in terms of 'dimensions', 'skills' and 'themes'. The latter are categorized as 'economic and industrial understanding', 'careers education and guidance', 'health education', 'education for citizenship' and 'environmental education'. This cross-curricular frame of reference, however, is overlaid on to an earlier frame which in no way anticipated the later accretion of 'themes', 'dimensions' and 'skills'. Indeed, in the wake of the Education Reform Act there would seem to have been an uncontrolled drift away from the hard-edged vocabulary of 'core' and 'foundation' subjects, comprising the 'basic' statutory curriculum, towards a more uncertain specification of other 'elements' whose status within the statutory curriculum is at the very least open to question.

Curriculum Guidance 3 remains conveniently silent on this issue, although the earlier *Circular 6* (NCC 1989), while stating that where the 'themes are embedded in the National Curriculum programmes of study they are statutory', goes on to state that 'other aspects, whilst not statutory, are clearly required if schools are to provide an education which promotes the aims defined in Section 1 of the Education Reform Act'. At no point, however, does either document state what these other aspects might be. There would seem, in other words, to be no intention on behalf of central government to define these aspects in terms of attainment targets and programmes of study outside those already existing within the 'basic' curriculum.

While teachers will no doubt breathe a sigh of relief at this unwonted diffidence, it does raise serious questions as to what exactly central government understands by curriculum coherence; particularly since, on past performance, commitments to particular curriculum priorities have been expressed as an urge towards legislative tidiness. (If it's important, render it statutory.) Those whose notion of coherence embraces something other than just a collection of subjects are bound to ask what exactly the National Curriculum is. Is it simply the 'basic' curriculum? Or does it include 'other aspects'? And, if the latter, is the National Curriculum legally binding? Such questions, of course, simply compound the muddle which the Education Reform Act ostensibly set out to clarify.

They also highlight the political problems attendant upon trying to introduce a more expansive notion of curriculum coherence into a debate from which it has so assiduously been excluded. The verb 'to cohere' – unlike so many of the key 'doing' words currently associated with curriculum development – is, significantly, intransitive: 'to organise', 'to structure', 'to design' all take 'the curriculum' as their object; 'to cohere' takes it solely as its subject. A curriculum cannot be *made* to cohere. Insofar as the notion of coherence is relevant, the curriculum must be seen as a process rather than as a product. Since that perspective has been so singularly lacking from government thinking, the late re-emergence of the notion of curriculum coherence through the back door of the NCC may be seen as an, albeit happy, illogicality.

The problem of overload

That illogicality does, however, give rise to some serious problems. Conventional wisdom would have us believe that the National Curriculum is not the whole curriculum. But, as Tim Brighouse and Philip Hunter (1990) have argued, 'that is an essential but insufficient understanding, for the National Curriculum is *more* than the whole curriculum also'. Even when conceived simply as the 'basic' curriculum of ten 'core' and 'foundation' subjects (with their imposing barrage of attainment targets and programmes of study) the National Curriculum is overcrowded. Add to that the 'other (unspecified) aspects' and one is landed with a serious case of curriculum overload.

This, of course, has financial and broader resource implications, which is no doubt one reason why the DES has belatedly

recognized that a problem exists at all. Having earlier acknowledged, at the Society of Education Officers' annual conference, that
there is a problem of overcrowding at key stage 4 (MacGregor
1990a), the then Secretary of State for Education went on record as
saying that there were 'legitimate worries about overload, about
over-assessment, about difficulties on the 14 to 16 age group and
how you get the whole of that quart into a curriculum pint pot'
(MacGregor 1990b). This was swiftly followed by an announcement at the annual conference of the Assistant Masters and Mistresses Association that the government had abandoned its plan to
introduce standard assessment tasks for 7-year-olds in all bar the
three core subjects (MacGregor 1990c).

The ministerial caution exercised by John MacGregor since
taking over the Department of Education and Science was in marked
contrast to the pioneering zeal of his predecessor, Kenneth Baker.
That contrast becomes all the more dramatic in the light of comments made by the then prime minister in the course of a lengthy
interview which, for one commentator at least, raised the question
of whether 'Mrs Thatcher's education policy [is] the policy which
is actually being enacted by the Government she leads' (O'Hear
1990). In the course of the interview the prime minister distinguished between 'the core curriculum' (of English, mathematics and
science) and 'the other things in the curriculum'. The former, she
claimed, 'is originally what I meant when we first started on this'. As
for the latter, she went on to say, 'I do not think I ever thought they
would do the syllabus in such detail as they are doing now' (Thatcher
1990).

Leaving aside that very odd use of the third person pronoun (Who
are 'they'? And who, other than 'we', gives 'them' the power to do
what 'they' are doing?), these comments are notable for the scant
regard they pay to the idea of 'the whole curriculum'. Insofar as
they imply any notion of coherence at all, they do so only on very
restricted terms: by wedding a back to basics approach (as far as
English, mathematics and science are concerned) with a distinctly
laissez-faire attitude towards 'the other things in the curriculum'.
One is left with the distinct feeling that, while the DES may have
jettisoned the notion of 'coherence' from that earlier HMI equation,
the prime minister of the day may not even have got as far as taking
on board the arguments for 'breadth and balance'.

Given these very different interpretations within central government regarding the nature of the National Curriculum, it is hardly

surprising that the guidance offered by the NCC on the composition of the whole curriculum is less than clear. The distinction between 'themes' and 'dimensions', for example, seems to be based on assumptions which are never made fully explicit and which are in any case open to question. Thus, health and environmental education, which are defined as 'themes', are assumed to have a strong component of specialized knowledge and understanding, while equal opportunities and multicultural education are seen as 'dimensions' which permeate every aspect of the curriculum and are the responsibility of all teachers. But is multicultural education necessarily any less knowledge-based than, say, environmental education and, if so, does this necessarily make permeation a less appropriate strategy for the development of the latter?

Cross-curriculum 'themes'

The basis upon which the five specified 'themes' have been selected is equally mystifying. *Curriculum Guidance 3* (NCC 1990a: 4) simply informs us that, although these constitute 'by no means a conclusive list', they 'seem to most people to be pre-eminent'. But this assumes a level of shared understanding which is manifestly lacking from the current debate. Some kind of consensus about the meaning of these 'themes' is, surely, a prerequisite of any coherent provision. Yet, as David Hargreaves (1990) points out, 'it is these areas of the curriculum where there is currently greatest diversity between schools'.

That diversity is apparent in the various meanings attached to the notion of 'education for citizenship'. As Maurice Roche (1987: 364) points out, 'in education systems awesome imponderables about the general nature of citizenship now and in the future must be regularly resolved, for good or ill, by Monday morning'. That is as may be, but in a recent national survey of secondary schools Ken Fogelman (1990) has shown that there is, in fact, wide variation in understanding of what the term actually means, while provision within the secondary school curriculum remains decidedly patchy. This may be partly the nature of the beast. After all, citizenship is a complex rather than a simple or unitary concept. Nevertheless, it is difficult to escape the feeling that, in spite of the NCC's faith in a national consensus, that Monday morning resolution is a somewhat partial affair.

One clear difference relates to the balance between rights and responsibilities: between 'the civil, political and social entitlements, and corresponding responsibilities of the individual in the community or state' (Morrell 1990). For those who place the emphasis on, for example, the European Convention on Human Rights and such other charters and conventions to which the UK is a signatory, much of what currently passes for citizenship education is little more than a training in how to become a useful subject. Conversely, the emphasis on 'active citizenship' is all too easily written off as political (i.e. Leftist) indoctrination by those for whom obligation and duty are the preeminent values.

Not surprisingly, the NCC attempts to engineer the appearance of consensus regarding this particular issue. 'Collective responsibility' is juxtaposed against 'rights and duties'; 'employment legislation' against 'trade unions'; even the phrase 'human rights' gets a look in (couched between 'international law' and 'planning'). Finally, in case the reader had not quite got the message, 'being a citizen – importance of participating; how to be involved' (NCC 1990a: 5). The array of buzz words and catch phrases presents a dizzy prospect.

The problems inherent in trying to build consensus from the top down in this way are amply illustrated by *Curriculum Guidance 4* (NCC 1990b), which is devoted entirely to the theme of 'economic and industrial understanding'. This document is equally meticulous in its attempt to balance the competing interests and viewpoints within what has become a politically sensitive field, and the guidance offered, although couched in the now familiar terminology of the enterprise culture, is broader and more liberal than one might have expected. Nevertheless, in reviewing the document, the press, almost without exception, announced its publication (on 2 May 1990) with headlines which totally ignored its attempt to achieve breadth and balance: 'Britain needs mini-Maggies in its schools' (*London Evening Standard*), 'Pupils should study business' (*The Guardian*), 'Entrepreneurs will start at five' (*The Times*) and 'Capitalists in the classroom' (*Daily Mail*).

Internal coherence

It would, of course, be grossly unfair to judge the effectiveness of NCC policy regarding 'the whole curriculum' according to a handful of newspaper headlines. The very crudity of those headlines, however, exposes the flimsiness of the supposed consensus upon which the document is based. Achieving curriculum coherence is clearly much more than just a matter of balancing competing terminologies and priorities within an overall statement of intent. It is also a matter of providing an evaluative framework within which teachers can begin to ascertain how, if at all, these good intentions add up in practice; how, that is, they translate into a set of learning experiences and what sense pupils make of those experiences.

Yet it is precisely this kind of framework which is missing from the perspective offered by the NCC Whole Curriculum Committee. According to that perspective, evaluation is but a single element within a broader category defined as 'curriculum audit' (NCC 1990a: 8–10). Again, the terminology is alienating and, in this case, misleading: what, after all, does evaluation have in common with the official scrutiny of accounts? Very little, unless it is reduced to a mere accountability exercise whereby 'current provision [is] to be matched against the curriculum requirements of ERA' (NCC 1990a: 8); in which case it is, arguably, not evaluation at all, but simply a means of ensuring that the curriculum has the appearance of a coherent whole, regardless of the contradictions and discontinuities that may be experienced by the pupils concerned. Any reclamation of a more substantial notion of curriculum coherence requires a re-examination of what it means to evaluate the whole curriculum.

That, however, involves a very different way of thinking about the whole curriculum; one, that is, in which coherence is defined in terms of the experience of the learner. This is not to deny in any way the importance of those other two elements in the curriculum equation (namely breadth and balance), which are more likely to be defined in terms of the sets of skills and bodies of knowledge associated with particular fields of study; but to affirm, rather, that a broad and balanced curriculum must appear to be so to those for whom it is designed. Only in this light can the curriculum be viewed as in any way whole.

Against the externally imposed notion of coherence (introduced through the National Curriculum) teachers need to reassert the notion of internal coherence (whereby the curriculum becomes coherent by relating to the whole experience of the learner). Curriculum evaluation, by focusing on this experience, can help those in schools articulate that notion and, in so doing, address their own professional need to go on learning about the process of learning itself and about what learning means to those they teach.

Any attempt to use evaluation to see the curriculum as all of a piece must, therefore, acknowledge that:

1 The whole curriculum is as much a matter of teaching methods and learning styles as of subject matter and content.
2 A curriculum may appear to have coherence on paper, and in the accounts offered by curriculum planners and policy makers, and yet fail to offer to particular pupils a coherent experience of learning.
3 As far as the individual pupil is concerned, the curriculum is a story, not a snapshot, and consequently must build over time as well as offer a coherent pattern of choices at any one point in the pupil's school career.

The kind of overview that we are seeking must, then, be centrally concerned with styles of teaching, with patterns of classroom organization, with the range of learning experiences on offer and with the wide diversity of learning outcomes that might ensue. It must seek to probe, not simply reproduce, the current crop of educational clichés, such as 'active learning', 'problem solving', 'flexible learning', 'relevance' and the like; it must tell us what these mean, and how they might cohere, in the experience of the learner. Some of the ways in which evaluation can help provide this kind of overview are discussed below in terms of various procedures associated with the systematic observation of classroom practice.

Paired observation

The term 'classroom observation' fails to capture the active, interpretive nature of this process; but it does have the advantage of common usage. In thinking about classroom observation, the point needs emphasizing that its prime purpose is not the observation itself, but the attempt to relate what one is observing – one's own and others' classroom practice – to the values espoused by the practitioners concerned. A central feature of any collegial approach to evaluation is its capacity for helping teachers to look systematically at what is happening within their own classrooms and to relate these observations to their own beliefs regarding the nature and purpose of education.

The ideal is a system of paired observation, whereby colleagues with common interests can observe one another's lessons over a specified period. The time span will depend upon the circumstances and the purpose of the exercise and may vary from a couple of weeks to a year. Within that period the teachers concerned may focus upon a particular class or follow one another's development across classes. The exercise may also involve some co-teaching so that the teachers concerned are involved in planning and implementation as well as observation. Regardless of how it is organized, classroom observation relies upon, and at the same time enhances, the quality of the professional relationship between those involved.

From the outset, therefore, it is important that the paired teacher / observers negotiate an agreed focus. There is no point whatsoever, given the rich complexity of classroom life, in trying to observe everything or in observing something that is of no interest or concern to the person being observed. Whatever focus is selected needs to be discussed, clearly understood and periodically renegotiated by both parties as the enquiry progresses. This means that, in preparing for classroom observation, one needs to set aside ample time for discussion before and after each of the sessions being observed.

Where the observer is an outsider (for example, a colleague from another school or from an institution of higher education) there is an even greater need to agree at the outset the focus of the observation. Under such circumstances, a contract may need to be agreed so as to ensure that the nature of the partnership is seen in similar terms by the teacher and the outsider. Nick May and Alan Sigsworth (1987: 252–3) offer a useful example of such a contract which they themselves used within a particular classroom observation exercise:

> With the intention that the partnership be based on equal and shared responsibility, the following is agreed:
>
> *Focus of observation:* to be chosen by the teacher and discussed until the outsider feels that the brief is understood and that it is clearly enough articulated to shape the observation. The focus may be refined or redefined by the teacher as appropriate.
> *Method of observation:* to be discussed by the two partners in terms of suitability to the chosen focus and any constraints of the classroom situation. The method may be refined or modified, as appropriate, during the course of the partnership.
> *Observational record:* to consist of non-judgemental notes made by the outsider, preferably in a carbon-copy notebook so

that sets of notes are immediately available for both the teacher and the outsider to study.

Post-observation discussion: to be conducted as soon as possible after the observation. The outsider has the responsibility for making a summary of this discussion so that it is possible for both partners to recall, at their next meeting, where they had got to in their analysis and interpretation of the data presented in the observation record.

Formative or summative discussion of procedures: at any stage during the partnership, either partner should be free to take the initiative in calling for a review of the way that the partnership is working.

Confidentiality: the outsider guarantees to regard the observations, the observational records, and the discussions and summaries of discussion as confidential information.

In terms of time allocation, a simple rule to follow is that the less overall time there is available the narrower the focus required. If there were worlds enough and time, the observer could afford to try and take in everything. But there never is and the need for clarity is, as a result, always pressing. The initial focus may be something as simple as the first five minutes of the lesson: what happens as the class is settling down? Who sits where and with whom? How does the teacher introduce the topic? What is important is that the teacher and the observer have a common perception as to what is being observed and why.

Another possible focus might be the kinds of questions posed by the teacher in the course of the lesson. How do these questions function: as prods? As control mechanisms? As testing devices . . .? What prompts them: misbehaviour? Silence? Curiosity . . .? What results from them: talk? Bewilderment? Embarrassment . . .? It is impossible for even the most aware teacher to recall precisely what questions he or she asked, to whom and at what point in the lesson, not to mention the effect of these questions on individual pupils and on the dynamics of the group. An observant third party can, however, pick up on these points and, in so doing, extend, as it were, the teacher's peripheral vision.

An observer can also be indispensable in helping to build up a composite picture of collaborative small-group work. Though rewarding, such work is extremely demanding and a second pair of eyes can help the teacher understand more fully what is happening within a particular small group, what its needs are and what kinds of learning are taking place. It may also be possible within this kind of situation for teachers to act as observers for short periods within lessons that they are responsible for co-teaching, alternately teaching and observing as the need arises.

These are examples only, but they do illustrate the need for clarity of focus. Classroom observation is perhaps best conceived as a collaborative venture in which the participants lend one another vision: help one another, that is, to see the less immediately visible aspects of classroom life. The trade off is seeing more and seeing better. This emphasis on what we see, and how, is important if only because it gives the lie to the easy assumption that what is significant in the classroom is immediately apparent. Classroom observation is important because it uncovers – allows to emerge – the underlying complexity of what learning and teaching are all about.

Within the literature on classroom observation, a distinction is sometimes made between participant and non-participant observation. In terms of a collegial approach to evaluation this distinction is not particularly helpful, since within this context it is difficult to conceive of a genuinely non-participant observation. The observer, as we have seen, may well have to move in and out of the observer role when team-teaching with a colleague and, anyway, the observation is likely to be instrumental in shaping the style and emphasis of the teaching programme. To that extent at least, the observer may be seen as a major participant in the curriculum planning process. Against this traditional emphasis on the division of labour between observer and observed, it may be more useful to think of a flexible, give and take relationship in which teachers are able to move in and out of the observer role as the need arises.

Nevertheless, within that collegial relationship it is important to be clear at any one time as to what role one is adopting. When in the observer role, one ought to be as unobtrusive as possible. It is also important that the pupils understand the conventions governing these shifts of role. In my own experience pupils can accommodate themselves to these shifts with surprising equanimity. But they do need to be let in on the act. In particular, the purpose of classroom observation needs to be explained at the outset; namely, that it is in the interests of both teacher and taught, since it helps create a classroom environment in which everyone – including the teacher – becomes a learner.

Conceptual mapping

A number of detailed observation schemes have been developed whereby the observer notes, at regular intervals, dominant behaviours occurring within the classroom according to certain prespecified categories. (For examples of these see Flanders 1970; Simon and Boyer 1970 and 1974; Galton 1978; Croll 1986). Such schemes in the main, however, presuppose a particular kind of relationship between observer and observed and admit few of the contextual clues that might allow the opportunity for a more detailed analysis of the behaviours concerned. The published versions of these schemes have, moreover, been developed by outside researchers who are not primarily concerned with promoting a collegial approach to in-school evaluation. Whatever observational schemes are developed are best kept as open and airy as possible so as to allow for ample discussion and the identification by specific groups and institutions of key issues and concerns.

Some kind of conceptual patterning is, in fact, much more useful (and exciting) than a simple behavioural checklist and can relate directly to the kinds of questions teachers need to address in trying to understand the processes of teaching and learning within their own classrooms. Are there, for example, any general patterns to be discerned in the teacher's response to pupils' unsolicited questions – or in the kind of attention that the teacher pays to different groups within the class? Is there a determined pattern to classroom discourse – for example, teacher talk, then student talk, followed by teacher talk? Is there a pattern to the way in which the teacher moves around the classroom in relation to specific individuals and groups? And, if some fairly general patterns can be discerned, how do these relate to the overall values and intentions of the teachers concerned?

At a rather higher level of generality the University of Leeds national evaluation of the TVEI pilot came up with an interesting conceptual framework with which to analyse teaching styles. This consisted of two dimensions: the participation dimension and the realism dimension. The former identifies, from an initial study based on case studies in twelve schools, 'three styles of teaching, *controlled, framed* and *negotiated*, which reflect the extent to which the teacher retains control of content, learning activities and criteria, or cedes some of that control by negotiating with students' (Barnes *et al.* 1987a: 24–5). In the case of each of these three styles, key characteristics are defined in terms of content, focus, students' role, key concepts and methods (Table 4.1).

Table 4.1 Teaching styles: the participation dimension

	Closed	*Framed*	*Negotiated*
Content	Tightly controlled by teacher; not negotiable	Teacher controls topic, frames of reference and tasks; criteria made explicit	Discussed at each point; joint decisions
Focus	Authoritative knowledge and skills; simplified, monolithic	Stress on empirical testing; processes chosen by teacher; some legitimation of student ideas	Search for justifications and principles; strong legitimation of student ideas
Students' role	Acceptance; routine performance; little access to principles	Join in teacher's thinking; make hypotheses, set up tests; operate teacher's frame	Discuss goals and methods critically; share responsibility for frame and criteria
Key concepts	'Authority': the proper procedures and the right answers	'Access': to skills, processes, criteria	'Relevance': critical discussion of students' priorities
Methods	Exposition; worksheets (closed); note giving; individual exercises; routine practical work; teacher evaluates	Exposition, with discussion eliciting suggestions; individual/group problem solving; lists of tasks given; discussion of outcomes, but teacher adjudicates	Group and class discussion and decision making about goals and criteria; students plan and carry out work, make presentations, evaluate success

Source: Barnes *et al.* 1987a: 25.

The realism dimension relates to the notion of relevance and (from the same data base of twelve schools) suggests that any unit of the curriculum could be located 'at some point on a continuum of realism, using three sets of criteria: the degree to which the knowledge and skills learnt are placed in a context, the extent to which the students accept the activity as realistic,

Table 4.2 Teaching styles: the realism dimension

	Routine relevance	*Explicit relevance*
Context	Skills out of context; students must accept tasks on the teacher's authority; routine exercises	Skills in a justificatory context; context displays purposes, criteria, relationship to other concerns and priorities
Source	Teacher owns the problem; skills and knowledge taught as answers to unasked questions; relevance not made explicit	Teacher designs situations that pose problems; or supports students' problem finding; students recognize problems before solutions offered; relevances enacted in advance
Tasks	Simplified, pre-analysed tasks; routine sequences; 'well-formed' problems with 'right answers'	Tasks are complex, 'noisy', not simplified; criteria for success are uncertain or contradictory; different methods seem possible and need investigation
Accounts	Accounts of phenomena are uncontroversial, uncritical, 'textbook' simplifications, avoiding complexity and dispute	Alternative accounts are acknowledged and criticized; different interpretations and conflicts of purpose are analysed and evaluated

Source: Barnes *et al.* 1987a: 32.

and the complexity of the tasks' (Barnes *et al.* 1987a: 31), (Table 4.2).

Placing these dimensional categories side by side provides a framework within which to discuss and analyse specific instances of classroom practice. It enables teachers to locate those points at which their pupils are, in all likelihood, taking responsibility for their own learning and thereby making the curriculum add up to something relevant and significant. It helps schools to think about how and why the curriculum is working – hanging together, cohering – at those precise points. It offers, in a way that simple behavioural checklists cannot, a perspective on the whole curriculum (see also, Barnes *et al.* 1987b and 1989).

Stories not snapshots

What is important in adopting such a perspective is not the accumulation of snapshots, but what those snapshots, when juxtaposed, tell us about discontinuity and connection, about dislocation and coherence; and not only across the organized, formal curriculum, but between that curriculum and what the young person brings to it. What is important is the 'coherence-in-the-experience-of-the-pupil' (Hargreaves 1987: 10): that, together with the communal culture that frames, but never quite determines, the individual – and individualized – experience of learning.

Pupil tracking

There are a couple of ways into these kinds of storylines, one of which is a particular observational technique known as 'pupil tracking'. Colin Hodgson makes a distinction between two kinds of 'tracking' exercise:

> Individual pupil, pupils or class 'followed' over a period of time by an observer who records observations using a checklist which defines the areas of interest;
>
> pupil, pupils or class 'recorded' by every teacher who teaches them over a period of time, using a checklist.
>
> (1990: 21)

One school, which has left a useful record of a particular tracking exercise, combined these two approaches by involving a group of five teachers in tracking individual pupils over a three-day period. Pupils were drawn from two distinct year groups:

> We wanted an equal number of boys and girls, some pupils from different cultural backgrounds and the pupils were to represent a cross section of ability. With these criteria in mind we would choose a pupil from each tutor group in the second and fourth year. Work was done to draw up an initial sample of pupils. Standardised Maths and English scores were used to try and achieve a mix of ability. We tried, especially with the fourth years, to achieve a mix of attitude.
>
> (Challis *et al.* 1986: 9)

The teachers involved in the exercise also devised a checklist which consisted of a number of categories against which they agreed to note the behaviour of the pupils they were tracking on a minute by minute basis:

1 administration
2 waiting, ie start of lesson
3 waiting – attention during lessons
4 not involved
5 listening to teacher
6 observing
7 practical – physical
8 pupil/pupil talk about work
9 pupil/teacher talk
10 assessing work
11 reading – factual
12 reading – imaginative
13 writing – copying
14 writing – notes
15 writing – recording
16 writing – creative
17 practical – creative

(Challis *et al.* 1986: 30)

These categories proved difficult and raised many of the problems associated with the kind of behavioural checklist mentioned above. They were, as the team of teachers themselves acknowledged, insufficiently differentiated and contextualized and somewhat narrow in their range of reference. But because they were used consistently, they did allow for some comparison across the pupil groups as originally identified. They raised some important questions about styles of teaching and learning and gave the teachers involved in the exercise an opportunity to present these to the full staff of the school. In the main these questions worried away at the general impression gained during the tracking exercise that 'students' experience at present seems too passive' and, in doing so, began to map such concepts as 'negotiated' and 'active' learning, 'involvement' and 'participation', 'practical' and 'creative' work:

Do/should examinations dominate our curriculum and teaching strategies?
Do we know enough about what is taught and how it is taught in other curriculum areas?
Is there a place for more negotiated and active learning?

Do we involve students in enough oral work?

What education is going on in non-involvement time in lessons?

How important is group, practical and creative work?

Do we spend too much time talking at students?

How much do we actually know about how learning takes place?

How can we encourage more active participation?

(Challis *et al.* 1986: 58)

The resource implications of mounting a system of either paired observation or pupil tracking are considerable. For such a system to be effective, time needs to be set aside before the observation session, for preparatory discussion and, immediately afterwards, for preliminary analysis and debriefing. The precise timing of the observations needs, therefore, to be carefully thought through. It may be, for example, that a lesson immediately before or after lunch, or at the very end of the day, would allow the teachers concerned some time together to talk through the relevant issues. Whatever system is adopted, it should be recognized that talking about what has been observed is as important as the actual observation itself.

Analysis of 'products'

Another way of trying to see the curriculum as all of a piece is to look at it in terms of the range of pupil products that it generates. All too often these are seen merely as the objects of assessment: as a means, that is, of grading pupils either in relation to one another or in accordance with certain pre-specified criteria. This is an important process, but not without its limitations. To see pupils' work solely as an opportunity for assessment is rather like entering an art gallery and trying to grade individual works of art on a scale of one to ten. It can be done and some of us – whether in an art gallery or a classroom – find ourselves doing that kind of thing a lot of the time. But it is by no means the only, or even the most interesting, thing one can do with human artefacts. There is a point at which assessment can become an insensitive or, at the very least, inadequate response.

For a start we tend to associate assessment with a fairly narrow range of pupil 'products': mainly (but not exclusively) final draft writing, finished art and design and (occasionally) prepared oral work within formal settings. This means that many of the more ephemeral classroom 'products' – rough jottings, sketches, lists and the like – drop below the sightlines of the existing assessment system. While the recent emphasis on pupil records of achievement (together with the greater stress on coursework within GCSE) has helped broaden the range of assessment procedures, most of what pupils actually produce in schools remains invisible.

It would, of course, be quite impracticable to collect and retain all the work produced by all the pupils within a particular school. Nevertheless, pupils might well accumulate a selection of 'products' to enable them and their teachers to reflect upon their development and the range of activities they have engaged in. Teachers might, in addition, periodically review the full range of 'products' generated by, say, a single class within a single day. This kind of evaluation, particularly if it is related to a staff development exercise, can offer some useful insights into the learning that is taking place in the classroom, the ways in which the learners are ordering their thoughts and feelings, and the kinds of support that particular groups or individuals may require.

An analysis of pupil 'products' can also help us to understand more fully the processes which have generated them and thereby to discern any underlying patterns in the practice of teaching and learning. Faced with a range of such 'products' we might, for example, ask which were the result of tasks set by the teacher and which were the result of pupil self-direction. Which resulted from pre-planning and which were themselves part of the planning process? Which of them generated new insights and which confirmed, or recorded, insights already gained through instruction or classroom discussion? In trying to understand what the whole curriculum means to pupils, these questions are of considerable significance.

The record of achievement 'movement' helps us to address these kinds of questions but, as it is currently being developed, does not go far enough. What is needed, at the very least, is a dossier of representative work (some in draft and some in final draft form) produced by individual pupils. A useful analogy is the artist's portfolio, which offers examples of very different kinds of work. Within the context of the National Curriculum, the student's portfolio ought, similarly, to offer a sample of different kinds of artefact produced by the student at different stages of development.

A useful preliminary exercise is for teachers to begin to categorize the kinds of pupil 'products' generated within their own subject area. A group of English teachers, for example, working within a particular year group of a particular school produced the following list drawn from the work collected in their classrooms within a single week:

- 'brainstorming' lists;
- essays;
- reviews;
- records of discussions;
- play scripts;
- stories;
- monologues;
- lists;
- diagrams;
- cartoons;
- letters;
- instructions;
- poems.

This, of course, is by no means an exhaustive list of the kinds of work produced within English studies generally. But it is an accurate list, as far as these teachers were concerned, of the work produced within their own classrooms over the period of a single week. As such, it raises important questions, for them, about the range and scope of the tasks set and about what English studies might mean for the pupils they teach. Moreover, in reaching beyond that list to the actual artefacts themselves, it enables the teachers to raise questions about quality and individual preference that, when explored, may shed further light on the pupils' experience of learning.

Similar lists, with significant variations, could be drawn up by teachers of different subjects, and similar questions addressed, as a way of understanding how the curriculum is understood by the pupils concerned. At a more ambitious level, some attempt could be made to map the kinds of pupil 'product' generated across the whole curriculum. How, for example, does the above list compare with the range of work produced in mathematics, science or art? What connections, overlaps, discontinuities are there? And what significance, if any, do these have? By exploring such questions, teachers can reach behind pupil 'product' to pedagogical process and so begin to question their own classroom, and departmental (or faculty), practice.

This kind of approach, of course, creates a considerable problem in terms of storage and retrieval. A number of schools, however, are beginning to overcome this problem by filing pupil portfolios in appropriate centres. These may be department or faculty rooms or, more usually, pastoral (house or year) rooms. Their importance as a focus for guidance and tutorial work cannot be overestimated. The pupil who is able to walk into her or his house room and consult an individual file containing a sample of work produced throughout the years of compulsory schooling gains an immediate sense of continuity and progression and, importantly, is able to track her or his own discontinuities and gaps. Such a system can also help knit together the pastoral and academic structures of the school and provide a basis for informed discussion between pupils and tutorial staff regarding progress and future options.

Summary

The whole curriculum is a complex matrix. It involves understanding the range of experiences and options open to a variety of pupils, at any given time, across an eleven-year time span. This chapter has tried to open up some of the ways in which schools can begin to understand that matrix through examining the kinds of learning experiences and teaching styles that pupils are likely to be exposed to at different stages in their development. In particular, it has suggested that schools think in terms of a three-pronged strategy which includes paired classroom observation; pupil tracking; and the analysis of pupil 'products'. In the following chapter we shall be looking at how this strategy might be augmented by the use of specific outcome measures.

– 5 –

Outcome Measures

It is hardly surprising at a time when the curriculum is becoming increasingly assessment led and schools more accountable that there should be a renewed interest in examination data as a measure of school effectiveness. For pupil assessment, certainly within the National Curriculum, is related not only to outcomes, but to those outcomes that are assumed to be quantifiable. It is important to remind ourselves, therefore, that examination results are not the only quantifiable data available in schools: records of attendance and of post-school destinations also provide accessible sources of information, while in addition schools might find it useful to quantify the kinds of learning experiences and styles of teaching that are on offer to pupils. It is also important to remind ourselves that, even when concerned primarily with quantifiable data, in-school evaluation is never just an arithmetical exercise, but always involves using the numerical 'facts' that have been gathered to question existing assumptions and thereby sharpen our thinking about current policy and practice.

Progression and pupil assessment

The introduction of standardized testing schemes for all pupils at the ages of 7, 11 and 14 (in addition to the existing assessment procedures at the age of 16) may well result in an orgy of counting, during which invidious comparisons (between individual pupils, between subject departments and between schools) will be constructed on slender and largely misunderstood evidence. The pressure on teachers, policy makers and governors to participate in these excesses is, moreover, likely to be acute. If they are to withstand them, they will have to become increasingly sophisticated in their interrogation of the evidence which the newly established assessment procedures place so beguilingly at their disposal.

In so doing, they might well heed Marten Shipman's (1979: 87) time-worn advice that 'the valid interpretation of examination results depends on allowing for factors outside actual teaching that might account for changes across the years or between subjects, or between a school and others'; and, in particular, that 'measures of attainment at intake . . . are some check on the possibility that results may be due more to the characteristics of the pupils than to any policy of the school'. The difference the school makes is, in other words, tangled up with other 'factors which seem to make a difference' (Gray 1990: 212).

There is an important issue here which John Gray (1982: 5) characterizes as 'standards versus progress'. A problem arises, he argues, 'when judgements in everyday language which are based on *standards* that have been reached are confounded with judgements that should be based on the *progress* pupils have made'. In order to make an informed judgement regarding the school's contribution one needs to know 'how much the *school* has added to the progress the pupils would have made, regardless of which particular school he or she attended' (original emphases). Clearly, in making such judgements, information regarding the prior attainment of pupils is crucial.

We can begin to see the relevance of this insight by considering a hypothetical group of pupils whose performance at key stage 4 differs markedly from their performance at key stage 2. To measure the achievement of such a group against a national norm could be extremely misleading. If, for example, the performance of this group at key stage 4, though on average fairly high, were to be bunched around a narrower differential, the school in question might well ask itself whether that was because it had been failing to challenge its more able pupils or because it had been working wonders with those who (according to prior measures) were less able. Only by checking the results against the pupils' prior performance scores could we make any sensible judgement regarding the significance of their current attainments.

This example also highlights the defects of using the sum of percentage pass rates as the main indicator of pupil achievement. These defects are usefully summarized by Carol T. Fitz-Gibbon (1990: 58–60). For the purposes of the present argument, however, it is sufficient to remind ourselves of three of her main points:

> When percentage pass rates are used, the focus is purely on the pass/fail dichotomy. Since we know that the level of a pass is important to people who use the results (e.g. employers and selectors for higher education) the reliance on a simple dichotomy is unjustifiable.
>
> If passes are added up from all subjects information about the different departments in the school is lost.
>
> Percentage pass rates . . . may push institutions to allow only potentially successful candidates to attempt some examinations such as A-levels. By only taking on students who seem sure to pass, the pass rate can be kept high.

Simply recording the percentage pass rates means, therefore, not only that no account is taken of the kinds of pupils entered (and therefore no adjustment made for intake), but that barely passing is counted in the same way as getting a high grade, that valuable information about the different departments in a school is lost and that 'a distorting effect on educational practice may occur' (Fitz-Gibbon 1990: 59).

These are serious drawbacks which can only be overcome by developing a more sophisticated system whereby results other than percentage pass rates are recorded. Reed Gamble (1990: 21), an adviser for Cleveland LEA, suggests, for example, a system based upon the following categories:

> % of 5th-year cohort to obtain four or more higher grades in GCSE.
> % of 5th-year cohort who obtain one or more higher grades in GCSE.
> % of 5th-year cohort who obtain four or more grades in GCSE.
> % of 5th-year cohort who obtain both maths and English higher grade in GCSE (note other core and foundation subjects to be included at a later date in line with introduction of National Curriculum).

% of 5th-year cohort who obtain other nationally accredited qualifications.

At the end of the day, whatever progress (or lack of it) that might be perceived to have been made cannot be attributable entirely to the school effect. But by taking into account measures of prior attainment, and going beyond a crude measure of percentage pass rates, schools are able to push their analyses forward so as to look at how well they are doing by pupils with very different sets of needs and expectations: they are able to make finer distinctions and more discriminating evaluative judgements. And that is of great importance.

Nevertheless, the use of prior performance data in the analysis of standardized assessment scores requires considerable circumspection. It is essential, for example, that the school should be comparing like with like; that the comparison, in other words, should 'be based on equivalent units computed in the same way (e.g. the number of passes per pupil rather than the total number of passes for the school)'. It is also important to bear in mind that 'the most likely reason for supposing that the results might differ from year to year is that the intake to the school has somehow changed'. (Gray 1982: 13). In the past most schools may have assumed that their intake remained constant over time; one beneficial (if unforeseen) consequence of the introduction of SATs is that such assumptions will be put, quite literally, to the test.

Where a school decides that the improvement (or otherwise) in pupils' overall performance is not attributable to differences in intake, it might well ask itself what the differences are attributable to. This raises a number of questions. For example:

> Has the change resulted from some deliberate change of school policy towards examinations? Are more pupils studying for more exams? Or could it be that the teachers have themselves become more effective at preparing their pupils?
>
> (Gray 1982: 15)

Although predating the 1988 legislation by more than half a decade, these questions still have a sting in the tail. It may well be, for example, that (as suggested by the first question) the establishment of a rolling programme of assessment for all pupils at 7, 11 and 14 (in addition to the public examination system at 16 +) will itself have an effect on pupils' measured attainment. It is also likely that such a programme will affect different children in different ways, not all of which will be beneficial. Such a system, which might naively be assumed to be an independent measure of the school effect, could itself prove to be a significant contribution to whatever influence the school exerts upon the child.

Given the changing pattern of public examinations, that second question (as to whether improvement in pupils' overall performance is a result of more students studying for more examinations) is also relevant. It would be interesting to see, for example, whether within particular geographical areas there was any correlation over time between patterns of unemployment, staying on rates and an increase in the number of pupils being entered for examinations at 16 + (see for example, Sime 1991). These kinds of broader social factors need to be considered when interpreting patterns and trends across the available data derived from raw assessment scores.

Since teachers are going to be spending that much more of their time in administering assessment tasks, the question as to whether they themselves have become more proficient at preparing their pupils for such tasks (a variant of Gray's third question above) is of considerable consequence. There is a very real danger of teachers, with the best of intentions, focusing within the foundation subjects, in particular, on attainment targets at the expense of the specified programmes of study. Where this occurs, it could undoubtedly skew the assessment results towards a perceived pattern of improvement without having any real impact on the overall quality of learning within the classroom.

This must remain a very important reservation in any serious attempt to use the results of pupil assessment for the purposes of in-school evaluation. For example, to use them for the purpose of comparing the quality of teaching within different teaching groups could well be misguided. Clearly, comparisons in respect of teaching quality need to be made; but they ought not to be based on assessment data alone. For these tell us very little about what in this particular instance we want to know. At best they highlight some very general questions (not necessarily about the quality of individual teachers, but about teaching styles, pupil intake, home background, etc.); questions such as, what is it about classroom x that produces this particular set of results? What happens in classroom y to produce these interestingly different results?

These questions can be sharpened, but not answered, by recourse to evidence relating to pupils' prior attainment. If, for example, we know that classroom x, although having fairly mediocre results generally, has done particularly well by its less able pupils, we shall want to know why. And if classroom y has produced results which, overall, are above average, but which on closer inspection reveal little progress among the least able pupils in the class, we shall want to know how this has come about. 'So examination results', as Harry Torrance (1987: 193) points out, 'may tell us a little bit about what has happened, but not how or why.' For that we must go to other kinds of evidence. (The kinds that are discussed in the preceding and proceeding chapters.) 'Results *per se* provide too little information, too late.'

There is something about examination results that calls forth a curious kind of dependency. That something is, of course, cultural and historical: part of an inherited and trained way of thinking that at certain crucial junctions blocks off the analytical option while appearing to fulfil it. Paul Valéry (1947: 74), in discussing words, wrote that 'our chief concern must be not to lean too heavily on them'. The same is true of numbers: of grades, marks, levels (whatever the terminology). Used wisely they provide a means of thinking about what happens in classrooms: of beginning to question the why and the how. Used unwisely, they run the risk of precipitating 'the most lucid of discussions . . . into a confusion of puzzling and delusive utterances which may or may not be charged with meaning'.

Attendance data

Next to examination results attendance records have, perhaps, the highest currency as far as hard data is concerned. For those who want instant (as opposed to discriminating) judgements on school effectiveness, rates of absenteeism provide a ready reckoner; provided, that is, that they are not analysed too closely.

Many of the reservations rehearsed in the previous section, in relation to examination data, also have relevance as far as attendance figures are concerned. In both cases the data requires careful contextualizing. But factors other than prior attainment come into effect here as well. Rates of absenteeism are, for example, 'closely related to the socio-economic background of the children entering the school' (Shipman 1979: 112). A recent report by HMI (1989: 43) adds an interesting, if enigmatic, gloss on this particular factor by suggesting 'that non-attendance rates correlate with variations in social background', while adding that 'many children from poor socio-economic backgrounds attend regularly and are not delinquent'.

That same report does, however, include some interesting examples of the ways in which schools can begin to analyse attendance data. These include:

- totalling an individual pupil's attendance by week and by half term;
- aggregating and averaging this for each class or tutor group;
- making comparisons of individuals, class or tutor groups and year groups, weekly and by term;
- providing more specific analysis of patterns of attendance for: *boys and girls*; *ability groupings*; *ethnic groupings*; *mornings and afternoons*;
- analysing the extent and incidence of intermittent non-attendance;
- analysing the extent and incidence of persistent non-attendance.

(original emphasis, HMI 1989: 13)

A more difficult task is to distinguish between types of absence. The most obvious distinction is between justified and unjustified absences; but, even where checking procedures are such as to allow schools to identify unjustified absences with some degree of confidence, this distinction alone ignores many forms of truancy which will not show up on routine register checks. 'Attending, registering, and then disappearing is one ploy' that Marten Shipman (1979: 111) draws attention to. 'Registering, but not attending classes is another. Selective attendance at classes is another.' Only by instituting a more elaborate system of checking attendance (both morning and afternoon; at the beginning of each lesson; unexpected spot checks) could schools begin to monitor these hidden forms of truancy.

Schools, however, face a real dilemma in setting up such a system. In order to encourage pupils to attend, schools need to create a warm, open and welcoming environment; an environment, that is, which may well be incompatible with the levels of surveillance necessary to keep an exhaustive check on truancy. The remedy, in other words, could all too easily aggravate the ailment. Most schools, quite rightly in my opinion, concentrate on recognizing and rewarding good attendance rather than tracking down every instance of lateness and truancy. Clearly, there are dangers inherent in this as in any other compromise; but these dangers can be minimized through close liaison with the educational welfare service and with a continuing regard for the causes of non-attendance among pupils.

As a young and inexperienced teacher working in an inner city comprehensive school, I remember being puzzled by the consistent lateness and occasional unexplained absence of a fourth-year pupil (Janice) whose attitude to her work was otherwise exemplary. On further investigation I learnt from an older and wiser colleague that the pupil in question was responsible for feeding and dressing her three younger brothers and sisters each morning and dropping one of them off at a neighbouring primary school. The latter was unable to receive her younger sister before half-past eight and, since it was a good quarter of a mile away from her own school which started at quarter to nine, some lateness was inevitable. None of this was the result of parental neglect. The only work the pupil's mother, a single parent, could obtain was a night shift ending at half-past seven in the morning. When the buses were on time, it took her just over half an hour to get home. By this time Janice had made breakfast, dressed the younger members of the family and set off for school with her younger sister.

Janice, of course, knew more about citizenship – about responsibility and loyalty – than is dreamt of in the NCC's (1990c) long-awaited *Curriculum Guidance 8*. But on paper – or rather in the register – she did have a problem. Instead of a neat row of diagonal lines (denoting unbroken attendance), she had a long list of 'lates', punctuated by the odd 'O' (denoting absence) when, because of a particularly late arrival, she had missed registration and gone straight to her first lesson. (At the end of each week dutiful form tutors placed an 'L' inside the 'O' against those pupils who, though absent for registration, had in fact attended lessons.)

This is a single example and cannot in itself begin to explain the widespread problem of non-attendance. It does, however, highlight the importance of trying to understand the causes that lie behind that problem and of acknowledging that some of those causes lie outside the school. Attendance, to draw on Marten Shipman's (1979: 113) wise words once again,

is only an indicator. It may indicate boredom or interest among pupils, or laxity or efficiency among staff, or the attraction of a subject, the effectiveness of pastoral care, or the fear of punishment. But it is probably always an incomplete and misleading indicator of anything specific. It is one piece of litmus paper, not a complete chemical analysis.

Some of the likely causes of non-attendance are in urgent need of enquiry. Equally, however, they often provide an extraordinarily difficult focus (methodologically and ethically) for in-school evaluation. How, for example, can a school explore the problem of bullying and of racial and sexual harassment that, for some pupils, may be a cause of truancy? To what extent should it pry into the personal circumstances of pupils and their families as a potential cause of irregular attendance? How can it highlight the problem of personality clashes between pupils and teachers as a possible cause of selective attendance at classes? There are no ready made answers to these questions, but any adequate response would depend upon a willingness to match quantitative with qualitative modes of enquiry; to reach behind the numerical record (of attendance, non-attendance and the like) to that other, more ill-defined record (of experience, parental support, material deprivation, etc.) that requires a different kind of reading. (See Gillborn, Nixon and Rudduck 1989.)

Destinations of school leavers

Until comparatively recently secondary schools have rarely kept systematic records of what happens to their pupils once they have left. The 'successes' were recorded: typically, on the wood-pannelled lists of graduates and prize winners that graced the corridors and assembly halls of the more academically self-conscious grammar schools. Some of the 'failures', too, found their way on to the unofficial record, by way of gossip, folklore and that still powerful determinant, 'reputation'. But, in the main, the destinations of school leavers remained unrecorded and unremarked.

That was no doubt partly because under a selective system of state education, whereby routes were largely predetermined at 11 +, destinations were taken for granted. Bolstered by spectacularly inequitable allocations (Byrne 1974), that system offered few surprises: by the time you were 12 you knew pretty well what line you were on. There were exceptions, but in the main it was 'the 11-plus branching point that was decisive for class selection before the comprehensive movement supplanted the tripartite system' (Halsey, Heath and Ridge 1980: 146).

For the vast majority, then, the freedom offered by the 1944 Education Act was the 'freedom for a selected few to escape – a policy of selective educational embourgeoisement' (Halsey 1986: 144). The significance of the comprehensive movement was that it redefined equality of opportunity in terms of a very different notion of liberty; one closer, that is, to the idea of solidarity. Freedom, at any rate, had less to do with 'freedom for a selected few' than with the liberty of all. This, potentially at least, increased the complexity and variety of routes through the system and greatly complicated the perceived relation between origins and destinations.

The move towards this more radical notion of equal opportunities is not without its opposing forces (some of which find powerful expression in the policy framework established through the 1988 legislation). Nevertheless, in most areas the 11 + branching point is now less decisive than it was in terms of the reproduction of structural inequality. Teachers can no longer take for granted the specific route or pathway that a particular young person will pursue on leaving school. They have to begin the difficult task of remapping those routes, so as to identify individuals or groups currently within the school who may be at risk in any future labour market.

A school can usefully set about this task by ascertaining the percentage of:

- pupils who at 16 + opt to continue in full-time education – and, where relevant, the proportion of these staying on at the same school; transferring to another school; and enrolling at a tertiary college;
- school leavers entering full-time employment – and the proportion of these receiving some on the job training; and some off the job training;
- school leavers entering Youth Training;
- school leavers out of work – and the proportion of these waiting to take up the firm offer of Youth Training or employment; and still looking for work;
- school leavers going on to 'something else' – for example, voluntary, unwaged or part-time work.

These five categories (full-time education, full-time employment, Youth Training, unemployment, 'something else'), although a bare minimum, provide a useful and manageable data base from which to be able to track the destinations of school leavers. Moreover, once a system of this kind has been established, it can be elaborated when and if necessary so as to provide more detailed information on particular issues. Schools might, for example, want to know more about the kinds of courses opted for by those pupils who continue with full-time education or the nature of the full-time employment undertaken by those pupils who find work. It is relatively easy to build in further questions once the baselines have been established. What is important is that the system can be administered with relative ease year by year and that the data it generates can be analysed in the time available.

It is important, in carrying out this analysis, that schools relate the information they gather on the destination of each school leaver to information regarding her or his examination performance and attendance record. Additionally, it will certainly prove useful, in trying to understand the kinds of routes taken by school leavers, to record something of the social and cultural backgrounds of individual pupils. The problem here lies in the selection of indicators. Clearly, in order to track any implicit gender bias, it is necessary to record the sex of the school leaver. For similar reasons, some record of ethnic origins may be considered useful. Information regarding social background is more difficult, although eligibility for free school meals is increasingly used as a rough and ready indicator. Some schools may also choose to record parents' occupation (Shipman 1979: 150–6).

In building background information of this kind into the data base, schools need to think ahead to the sorts of questions they may want to ask in the future. If, for example, a school wants to look at the possible relation between parental involvement and post-16 routes, it will need to have gathered some information regarding levels of parental support. (A crude, though workable, indicator might be whether the pupil's parent/s or guardian/s attended the year 11 parent evening.) It will be too late, as far as the analysis of current data is concerned, to build new items into the system once the pupils have left. Schools need to work out in advance their broad lines of enquiry, so as to make sure of gathering the necessary background information on future school leavers.

Options and attitudes

The outcome measures we have considered so far – public assessment data, attendance records and post-16 routes and destinations

– relate only indirectly to the notion of curriculum coherence. The following measures relate more directly, in that they point to the pupil's own decisions about, and perceptions of, what constitutes a coherent curriculum. Coherence, after all, is not just a function of curriculum design; of whatever breadth and balance is on offer. It is also a function of the mind that is learning; of the sense students make of what is there to be learnt.

Option choice

There is no doubt that the National Curriculum, in an attempt to offer a broad and balanced education to all pupils, has reduced the range of options that was previously available to some pupils within some schools. Nevertheless, the system would seem to allow for greater pupil choice than was at first envisaged. What the NCC first suggested was that 'it should be properly left to schools to allocate time to subjects within a broad framework based on certain assumptions' (Graham 1990b). Those assumptions were that, at key stage 4, all pupils should study English, mathematics and science to GCSE; that all pupils should take a modern foreign language and technology to GCSE or equivalent; that all pupils should follow geography and history to GCSE with a combined course for those who do not wish to take them as separate subjects; and that there should be some study of the arts to GCSE or equivalent.

This went some way towards relieving the log jam at key stage 4. It was certainly more helpful than Duncan Graham's (1990a) earlier disingenuous statement on the subject; namely 'that the most exciting things will happen when secondary schools throw all the attainment targets in a heap on the floor and reassemble them'. Having benefited from what 'the best brains of NCC and others have been pondering long and deep', the chairman of the NCC was now of the opinion that 'within a framework of five subjects which all must take, and the recommendations for history, geography and the arts, lies very considerable flexibility for schools which could be used for additional study of the foundation subjects' (Graham 1990b).

Unfortunately, however, the newly appointed Secretary of State for Education disagreed with him as to the degree of flexibility that was required. In an attempt to loosen up the suggested framework, Kenneth Clarke (1991), in his statement to the North of England Education Conference, reinstituted a two-tier system, with both academic and vocational qualifications, and relegated art and music to optional extras. Schools, he pronounced, were to have the options of shortened courses (taking about half the time of GCSEs) in some subjects; courses combining subjects, whether through GCSE or new vocational options; and accelerated classes leading, possibly, to super GCSEs.

Precisely because this revised framework offers greater flexibility, it is liable to perpetuate certain undesirable patterns of pupil choice. The continuing debate on equal opportunities shows that curriculum choice is not always what it seems (see for example, Pratt, Bloomfield and Seale 1984) and that, as one of the recent contributors to that debate has argued, the transition from year 9 to year 10 still represents 'a key decision making stage where factors other than ability may influence the direction of future success or failure' (Gillborn 1990: 161). This is not an argument against flexibility, but a reminder that the options offered by a school and the choices that are made by its pupils require careful and continuing evaluation.

It should also be borne in mind that, while the National Curriculum may have reduced the occasions on which pupils have to choose between courses, many of the styles of teaching that have gained credence over the last ten years have greatly increased the occasions on which pupils have to make choices within those courses. Indeed, the premium placed upon pupil choice might be seen as one of the main unifying themes running through a wide range of current practice (variously described as 'problem solving', 'active learning', 'independent learning', 'cooperative group work', etc.). It is necessary, therefore, in thinking about patterns of pupil choice to examine carefully the kinds of decisions that pupils make in the classroom and how those decisions influence the tasks that are set, the knowledge that is gained and the skills that are acquired.

Resetting the problem in this way makes it less easy to identify readily available outcome measures. The number and complexity of decisions that are taken by a class of pupils whose teacher places a high premium on pupil choice are likely to defy calculation. Nevertheless, it is possible over time to track some of the more important decisions that pupils take (regarding for example, the kinds of assignments undertaken and the materials used), so as to keep a check on any possible gender bias or any lack of balance inherent in the overall pattern of pupil choice.

This kind of evaluative exercise is highly relevant to the notion of curriculum coherence, since it is what pupils bring to their learning (in terms of the options taken and the decisions made) that render it coherent. At the same time, however, schools have a responsibility to ensure that what coheres for the individual pupil has the breadth and balance that characterizes the whole curriculum. Understanding how pupil choice is operating across the full range of curriculum and pedagogical options can help schools to get that equation right.

Attitude surveys

Given the current emphasis on increased pupil participation and negotiation, it is, as Richard Hazelwood (1990: 72) points out, 'remarkable that few attempts are being made systematically to examine pupil attitudes to schooling'. This may be because, in the past, such attempts have tended to employ highly specialized psychometric instruments within a programme of pre- and post-testing in which the 'experimental' group of pupils was clearly distinguished from the 'control' group. Not surprisingly, many teachers now find such an approach intrusive, potentially divisive, ethically questionable – and, of course, hopelessly time consuming.

It is possible, however, to gather useful information on pupil reactions to lessons and courses without going down that particular path. Indeed, most of what one needs to know in order to set about gathering some such information can be summed up in three simple 'rules' – the three Rs – governing the design of in-house questionnaires.

1 *Readability*
  The pupils for whom the questionnaire is designed must be able to read and understand it. This is such a seemingly basic point that it may appear patronizing to mention it. In fact, however, it is often overlooked or at least not given sufficient attention. Because teachers share a working environment – the classroom – with their pupils, it is all too easy to assume that they also share a terminology with which to describe it. Pupils, however, may have little understanding of terms which, because frequently used by teachers, hardly seem to them part of a technical or specialist language. Keep it simple.
2 *Reliability*
  The items comprising the questionnaire must be such as to yield reliable information relevant to the focus of the enquiry. Again, this point is by no means as straightforward as may at first

appear. Suppose, for example, the focus is on pupil attitudes to a particular course of study. Simply to ask pupils whether or not they enjoy the course may tell us very little, other than how they were feeling, for whatever reason, when they filled in the questionnaire. Judgements regarding pupil attitudes should always be based on a number of items, some of which may contradict or duplicate one another, so as to provide an internal check. Wherever possible anonymize questionnaires, so as to encourage greater honesty.

3 *Replicability*

Any questionnaire should be such as to allow for some replication, if this is considered necessary or appropriate. It could, for example, be applied to the same group of pupils at a later stage of schooling or to a different group undergoing the same course. This could reveal some insights into patterns of progress (both among pupils and within the course), though it would be unwise to read too much into evidence of this kind, given the variety of factors affecting pupil attitudes. The simpler the questionnaire is to administer and process, the more likely it is to become part of a recurring cycle of monitoring and evaluation.

These points apply also to the gathering of information on teacher attitudes and perceptions; regarding, for example, the adequacy of some aspect of school policy or the quality of school-focused INSET provision within the school (see Nixon 1989c: 49–59). Any group attempting to gather this kind of information would do well, however, to heed Rob Walker's (1985: 101–2) advice on the use of questionnaires in what he terms 'small-scale intimate settings'. Within such settings, suggests Walker,

> questionnaires . . . can be used with a sense of risk that would not be possible when they are used for collecting responses from large samples through direct mailing or by making use of trained interviewers. This is possible because in face-to-face contact there are opportunities for cross-checking, fast turnaround of information and generally a higher redundancy in communication than is present when the researcher faces large quantities of anonymous returns. This is perhaps why many of the standard texts on questionnaire design, while they offer much advice that is appropriate, are sometimes pitched at a level of precision that is inappropriate for the designer of a small-scale study.

Summary

This chapter has reviewed five useful and fairly accessible sources of evaluation evidence: national testing and examination results, attendance records, information on school leavers, pupil option patterns within and across courses, and pupil and teacher attitudes. Although each of these generates quantitative information, each also raises issues and questions that can only be fully explored through the use of more qualitative data gathering methods. In considering the kinds of evidence derived from interview and the means of gathering such evidence, the following chapter presents one such method, not as an alternative, but as a complement to the qualitative and quantitative methods already outlined in this and the previous chapter.

− 6 −

Interview Evidence

Evidence derived from interview can provide vital information, not only about what is happening in schools and classrooms, but about what pupils, parents, teachers and others think and feel is happening. Indeed, the interview acknowledges that those thoughts and feelings are themselves part of what is happening; that in order to grasp the curriculum as a coherent whole it is important to understand what sense, if any, pupils are making of their own learning and what meaning schools have for the teachers who work in them and for the local communities of which they are a part. Methodologically, therefore, the interview is an indispensable bridge between the particular approach to evaluation advocated within this book and the particular notion of curriculum coherence that underpins it.

Kinds of interviews

Interviews are traditionally categorized in terms of the extent to which the form and sequence of the questions asked are pre-specified. It is in this sense that Louis Cohen and Lawrence Manion (1980: 243) distinguish between structured and unstructured interviews:

> The structured interview is one in which the content and procedures are organized in advance. This means that the

sequence and wording of the questions are determined by means of a schedule and the interviewer is left little freedom to make modifications. Where some leeway is granted him, it too is specified in advance. It is therefore characterized by being a *closed* situation. In contrast to it in this respect, the unstructured interview is an *open* situation, having greater flexibility and freedom . . . Although the research purposes govern the questions asked, their content, sequence and wording are entirely in the hands of the interviewer.

Between these two sharply distinguished types is a third type: the semi-structured interview. This is a very broad category and includes, for example:

- interviews in which the wording of the questions is pre-specified, but their sequence allowed to vary;
- interviews in which both the wording and sequence of the questions varies, though the key issues to be covered are pre-specified; and
- interviews in which sequence (storyline, autobiography, history, etc.) provide the only pre-specified element.

How and to what extent the interview is pre-planned will depend to a great extent on the purpose of the exercise and the constraints that are operating. Evidence derived from more unstructured interviews generally takes longer to process (particularly if more than one interviewer is involved), since the organizing categories have to be constructed and cannot be assumed. On the other hand, the more heavily structured interview runs the risk of simply telling us what we already know.

It is worth bearing in mind the extent to which the interview, as a distinct cultural form, now pervades everyday life. Anyone conducting an interview, or being interviewed, is doing so against a backdrop of television chat shows, news reporting and continual media coverage in which the interview plays a highly significant part. Sometimes people refer to the 'research interview' as if it were in a different world from all this other, more 'journalistic' information gathering activity. But, of course, it is not and cannot be. The expectations of the interviewee, the style adopted by the interviewer, and the conventions governing their interactions are all embedded within that more extensive grid of codes.

Acknowledging this continuity of usage helps us to understand something of the immense versatility and variety of the interview form. To see it as stretched out between two fixed points – the structured and the unstructured – is ultimately not very helpful. What is important is to grasp something of the breadth of its application, so that it can be adopted appropriately and sensitively in different contexts. The structure of any interview is determined not only by the extent to which (and manner in which) the questions are pre-specified, but by the identity of the interviewer and interviewee, the relationship between them, and the nature of the situation in which the interview is being conducted. In that sense at least, no interview is unstructured to the evaluator who wants do a good job.

In preparing for an interview (as opposed to simply deciding on the content, sequence and wording of the questions), it is therefore useful to consider carefully the particular interview group involved and their relationship with the interviewer. For example, an interview conducted by a headteacher with members of her or his own staff is likely to be a very different kind of thing (even if the questions are identical) from an interview between two classroom teachers who have worked closely together on a joint project. (And, interestingly, each of these is different again from that almost nightly spectacle: a rushed interview with a senior cabinet minister conducted by an up and coming though still fairly inexperienced news reporter.) Status matters because it implies power; and power, insofar as it is unequally distributed, renders dialogue that much more difficult.

This is not to say that the element of power can be eradicated from the relationship between interviewer and interviewee. The interview is framed by an institutional context which, certainly in the case of educational evaluation, is highly ordered and often finely stratified. To imagine that the research interview, whether conducted by an insider or outsider, is somehow uncontaminated by these institutional factors is to live in cloud cuckoo land. It matters very much who is interviewing whom, where and when; a point that should be fully acknowledged, and its implications thought through, in preparing for any round of interviews.

Interviewing pupils

This point is particularly relevant when it comes to interviewing pupils. In an article that focuses upon the practice of interviewing in case study research and includes a useful section on interviewing pupils, Helen Simons (1981: 38) points out that:

> Pupils learn to live by rules and conventions prescribed by those responsible for the running of the school and may not *feel as free* as teachers to express their attitudes and feelings. In schools which have a fairly traditional curriculum, furthermore, pupils may not have had much opportunity to talk in class or informally to teachers outside class . . . Some pupils appear to treat the interview as a test situation, and try to give 'right' answers. (original emphasis)

This problem can be partially alleviated by ensuring that no pupil is under compulsion to be interviewed. Pupil interviews should be entirely and genuinely voluntary. There are sound pragmatic as well as ethical reasons for this, 'since where pupils have been selected by the teacher they may associate the interviewer with the authority structure and this may restrict discussion' (Simons 1981: 38). Even when pupils themselves volunteer, schools may choose to inform parents, or seek their agreement, prior to the interviews taking place. Clearly, this will depend to some extent on the age of the pupils concerned, but, regardless of age, the involvement and understanding of parents can only serve to strengthen the eventual impact of the evaluation.

Interviewing pupils in groups may also help to overcome any uneasiness or diffidence among the interviewees; provided, that is, that they know each other and have worked together in groups before. Where pupils do not know each other, or where the issues touched on are likely to be sensitive and potentially embarrassing, group interviews with pupils may, on the other hand, be counterproductive. The important thing is that each interviewee should feel as relaxed and at ease as possible. So again it is often simpler and most effective to let the pupils themselves decide how they would like to be interviewed and, if in groups, with whom.

In certain instances it may be appropriate to dispense with an interviewer altogether and ask the group of pupil 'interviewees' to talk around a number of questions on their own. Under these circumstances one of the interview group might be asked to act as chairperson so as to ensure that the questions are covered and that the group keeps to the task. This can be an extremely effective strategy with pupils who are skilled and experienced in small-group discussion and who have some specialist 'insider' knowledge of the issues being discussed. Pupils may, for example, be more willing and able to talk about their responses to a particular teaching style or activity if left to get on with it than if faced with an adult interviewer.

When this is attempted it is important to ensure, however, that the pupils are aware of, and comfortable with, the conventions; otherwise, as the following extract reveals, they can find themselves in quite a muddle. In this exchange Anthony has agreed to interview his friend, Adewole, about a course of drama lessons they have both attended. Both Anthony and Adewole are in the second year at a comprehensive secondary school.

Anthony: I'm going to ask 'Wole what he thinks. I'm going to be like an interviewer and I'm going to ask 'Wole different things about the lesson: you know, what he feels about it. The first question I'll ask him is what does he think drama is? What does he think he comes here to learn?

Adewole: I think I come here to learn, well, all sorts of things really: to learn how to do things properly, to play in a properly behaved manner, and most of all to become a film star I suppose. I want to be a film star when I grow up. Well, I suppose that's what drama is about, so you can act on telly and all those kinds of things.

Anthony: Now we're going to turn it into a conversation between us two. 'Wole, you said that you think you come here to learn to be a film star. That really isn't it though, is it? You don't really learn how to act. You don't learn *Romeo and Juliet* or anything like that. You come here really to learn how to be someone you aren't. To give out your feelings more.

Adewole: Yes?

Anthony: In drama, you just are being someone you aren't really. You're told to walk posh, you know, sort of stick your nose in the air.

Adewole: Like Marcia. (*another member of the drama group*)

Anthony: Yes, like Marcia. You walk along there and you see another person who has to act like a small person, you know, really tiny, to everybody else, and asking for food, and . . .

Adewole: A beggar.

Anthony: Yes, a beggar. The one who's acting posh has to go past that beggar and stick their nose up in the air, you know, really act like he's a, you know, and walk past.

Clearly, Anthony has very little interest in interviewing Adewole.

He has some strong views of his own and is keen to express these. Once this is acknowledged, the dialogue gathers momentum: Anthony stops referring to his friend in the third person and the exchange, to use Anthony's word, is much closer to a conversation. With the two friends working together to express a shared perception, the interview becomes a form with which they themselves can feel comfortable and can cope. It works, in the sense of generating interest and insight, because the pupils reject the conventions within which they feel they ought to be operating and begin to define more appropriate conventions for themselves. (For an account of the course of lessons discussed by Adewole and Anthony see Case study 7, Strategy C in Stenhouse *et al.* 1982: 204–19).

The size and composition of any interview group are also important considerations. In my experience, if the number of interviewees exceeds four, it is very difficult to disentangle individual voices and viewpoints and to ensure that everyone has a say: groups of two or three are probably ideal. There can be no hard and fast rule governing the composition of interview groups. However, it is probably better to avoid mixed groups of girls and boys and of pupils drawn from different age groups, since these groupings could introduce their own tensions and inhibitions. The point of interviewing in groups is, after all, to put pupils at their ease and to reduce as far as possible the sometimes inhibiting effect produced by the teacherly presence of an adult interviewer.

Using the 'outsider'

That effect can sometimes be reduced further by arranging for an outsider to conduct the interviews. This could be a colleague from another school or from a local institution of higher education. Either way it needs to be someone whom the staff trust, who can talk easily with young people, and who is sensitive to the kinds of issues on which the evaluation is trying to focus. Such individuals are rare and, even if located, may not have time to involve themselves in an evaluation exercise of this kind. Schools are, however, more likely to be able to draw on this kind of expertise if they see evaluation as a collaborative venture and, as a result, work at establishing and sustaining cross-institutional links.

Trust is essential. Having someone from outside the school interviewing pupils about some aspect of one's own teaching can, for example, be extremely threatening. As in the case of classroom observation, the focus of any such interview needs to be fully discussed in advance with all those concerned. Interviewees need to be clear from the outset as to how, and to whom, their comments are to be passed on and what feedback, if any, they themselves can expect to receive in return for giving up their time to be interviewed. If the interviews are taped, the interviewees also need to know what will happen to the tapes once the evaluation exercise has been completed. These could, for example, be filed for a limited length of time before being either erased or handed over to the interviewees.

In spite of these potential difficulties, the outsider is well placed to pick up on issues that, because of their familiarity, may all too easily be overlooked or dismissed as trivial by those who have to live with them. Such issues, as Rob Walker (1985: 157) points out,

> are most effectively identified by following any discrepancies that emerge: within the statements made by one person, between what people say and what they do, or between policy and practice. Sometimes they will be large-scale discrepancies – for example a school that has a policy of mixed-ability teaching apparently implementing forms of disguised streaming. They may be discrepancies at the level of classroom practice . . . Or they may be significant discontinuities encapsulated in a single utterance.

The single most valuable attribute of the outsider, as far as research and evaluation is concerned, is what, under other circumstances, makes being an outsider so difficult and stressful: the naivety and general lack of 'with-it-ness' attached to the role. Not knowing is tremendously important if the object of the exercise is to find out. As Miss Marple well knew, it allows one to ask questions that would otherwise be embarrassing in their simplicity; to broach, with impunity, topics that represent, to the initiated, complete no go areas; and to make connections that run counter to the received wisdom of the insiders. It is a powerful role, to be used with responsibility and tact.

Handling the form

All interviews have structure and form: even those in which the pre-specification of wording and sequencing is at a minimum. Indeed, the interviewer's concern with formal and structural matters is likely to be, if anything, more acute in those interviews that have a strong improvisatory element. In my own experience of conducting interviews in a wide variety of contexts and of studying the interview evidence gathered by colleagues, a number of formal requirements can be distinguished. These, I would argue, apply to any kind of interview, but demand the greatest skill in those that are ironically referred to as semi-structured.

Shaping

The first of these requirements is that any interview should have a sense of shape and continuity: a beginning, a middle and an end. This can be achieved, in part, by informing the interviewee beforehand as to the length of the interview, its likely phases, and the kinds of issues to be covered. In addition, however, it is important to keep on reinforcing the structure of the interview as it is being conducted. This can be done in a number of ways:

1 *Reflecting back*
   Periodically, the interviewer can reflect back to the interviewee what has just been said (e.g. 'I think what I'm hearing is . . . Have I got it about right?'). This can be a useful way of ensuring that, as interviewer, one is indeed understanding the point being made. It also, however, gives the interviewee an opportunity to stop and think and, if necessary, to sharpen or expand upon that point. When reflecting back in this way, the interviewer needs to be very tentative so as to ensure that he or she does not put words into the interviewee's mouth or inadvertently push the interviewee towards saying something more extreme than originally intended. Reflecting back is essentially a checking device, whereby the interviewer is confirmed in the role of active listener and the interviewee in the role of serious witness.

2 *Gathering*
   In order to round off one section of the interview and lead into the next, the interviewer can gather up the main themes that have been covered and invite the interviewee to add to, or if necessary modify, this interim summary. If, for example, the first part of an interview with a group of teachers had concentrated on aspects of the interviewees' previous classroom experience, the interviewer could try to characterize the key features of that experience before moving on to questions relating to the present. Again, great care needs to be taken not to falsify or elaborate what has

been said. When used sensitively, however, the gathering of key themes and issues, so as to mark a shift of focus or emphasis within the interview, can be a useful procedural device.

3 *Signalling*

It can be helpful to signal, early on, the kinds of questions that are to be posed later in the interview. This serves a number of purposes: it reminds interviewees of the ground to be covered, enables them to offer more relevant replies, and deters them from churning out a set response regardless of the question asked. Frequently, in my experience, interviewees will themselves request such a signal, by asking whether this is the appropriate point to introduce a particular topic. ('Do you want me to talk about this now, or are you going on to that later?') It should be added that this device is easily misused; as when, for example, it serves to block an unforeseen argument or an unexpected insight.

Focusing

A second formal requirement of the interview is that it should have a clear sense of focus. This can be achieved partly by ensuring beforehand that interviewees understand what it is they are to be interviewed about and why. It is important also, however, that as the interview progresses the interviewer and interviewee each feels that he or she is talking in terms that the other can understand; that the interview, in other words, is taking place within a common frame of reference. There are, again, a number of ways in which a common frame of this kind can be established so as to ensure that the interview is in focus:

1 *Recollections*

An interview, or part of one, can, for example, focus upon a specific case or instance drawn from the interviewee's memory. That case could be a lesson or part of a lesson, a particular interaction with a pupil or colleague, a difficult or challenging moment in the classroom, etc. The interviewee is asked to recall the instance in question (this may take several minutes of silent reflection) and briefly describe it. This recollection is then used as the basis for further questioning, so as to draw out its significance. When the recollection is of an experience which both the interviewer and interviewee shared, it is important to ensure that the focus remains on the interviewee's perceptions as opposed to those of the interviewer.

2 *Materials*
Certain kinds of materials can fulfil a similar function. Interviews with pupils, for example, can usefully focus on work they themselves have produced or on teaching materials that have been presented to them. Similarly, interviews with teachers can focus on lesson notes, policy documents, pupils' work, etc. Very often materials of this kind simply provide a starting point, with follow up questions leading to more general issues and concerns. They can ensure, however, that the starting point at least is secure and that the interviewee has something tangible and unthreatening to refer to at the outset.

3 *Images*
Some kinds of visual images can also provide a strong focal point for the interview: notably, perhaps, photographs, but other kinds of images, too, that symbolize or evoke key aspects of the particular theme being explored. When interviewing pupils about a particular course of lessons, I have, for example, sometimes placed on a table beside the interviewee some of the tools or utensils associated with those lessons: a paintbrush, say, and a lump of clay; or a ruler and a pocket calculator. These can themselves provide a valuable lead in but, more important, act as a reminder that the interview is about something material in the interviewee's own experience.

Deepening

A third requirement is that the interview should nudge the interviewee towards a deeper analysis of the issues that are being raised. This calls for a gently challenging manner, whereby problems and queries are put to the interviewee with a view to eliciting a clearer statement of her or his value position. In my experience, certain kinds of questions prove particularly effective in this respect:

1 *What if?*
'What if' questions pose the interviewee with hypothetical situations which serve to test her or his assumptions. The 'what if' may refer to an event ('So what would you do if such and such occurred?'), a perspective ('How do you think you might have reacted if you'd been so-and so?'), an outcome ('What would you

feel about that if the consequences had been very different?') or whatever. They should never appear to be trick questions or be designed to catch interviewees out. In posing a 'what if' question, the interviewer is inviting the interviewee to be thoughtful and speculative, reflective and analytical.

2 *Present as past*

A similar effect can be achieved by inviting the interviewee to look at her or his present situation as if in extended retrospect. Looking at situations in this way (ie as if one is looking back on them after, say, five or ten years) can help to highlight what is important or significant about them. When interviewing pupils about their experience of schooling, I often, for example, ask them what, in ten years time, they think they will look back on with a sense of pride/disappointment/resentment/etc. In responding to such a question interviewees are having to think carefully about both the situation and their own response to it.

3 *What next?*

Asking interviewees 'What next?' (what consequences might follow from a particular decision they have taken, for example, or what influences might affect a particular course of action) provides another opportunity for reflection and analysis. It requires the interviewee to stop and think (about context as well as sequence, change as well as continuity) and, as such, deepens and extends the interview. In looking ahead, the interviewee is necessarily taking stock of the past and the present.

The points mentioned above are, it should be emphasized, only examples and represent a personal, not to say somewhat idiosyncratic, approach to interviewing. Any experienced interviewer develops a distinctive style which includes some favourite and well tried questions, particular ways of handling the transition from one topic to another within the interview, and strategies for digging beneath the interviewee's stock responses. Regardless of the extent to which the wording and sequencing of the questions is determined beforehand, these stylistic features are an important means of providing a sense of structure.

They are also a means of ensuring that the interview is, if at all possible, a valuable experience for the interviewee. This is an important consideration in any approach to evaluation which aspires to be collegial. The thought of being interviewed can for some people be a threatening prospect. If handled sensitively, however, the interview form can offer a rare opportunity to reflect upon aspects of one's own practice. Every effort should be made to ensure that the experience is as positive and rewarding as possible. It may, for at least some interviewees, be one of the very few occasions on which they are listened to intently for a sustained period on matters relating to their own experience of schooling.

Patterns, themes and issues

Interviews can generate an immense amount of data. Serious thought needs to be given, therefore, to the length of each interview and to the number of interviewees. Where interviews are taped (and this is advisable since otherwise so much is lost, including the interviewee's voice), some system may need to be devised whereby only selected passages from the tape are transcribed. To transcribe interviews in their entirety can be extremely time consuming (and therefore expensive). It can also be wasteful of effort. Transcription is, after all, a fairly mechanical task, whereas the selection of relevant passages involves some element of analysis.

In reviewing evidence gathered through interview one is looking for common patterns of response, for differences of opinion and perspective between interviewees, and for significant discrepancies within and across responses. Rarely can such analyses be usefully quantified. Interviews tend to highlight shades of difference, rather than polarizations; broad similarities and general agreements, rather than identical standpoints. Any attempt to reduce these subtleties to a head count of for and against, even if it were desirable, is likely to be impossible in practice.

This means that great sensitivity is required in the reporting of interview evidence. Because of the difficulty of quantifying fine shades of opinion, general comparative terms (more and most, less and least) have to carry a heavy semantic load and should be used with great care. Where minority viewpoints are reported (particularly when these are critical) some indication should be given of their general level of support among those interviewed. Similarly, the exceptional one off insight or occurrence should certainly be acknowledged, but needs to be carefully set in context. Misrepresentation can occur, not only through misquotation, but through a failure to achieve a sense of balance and proportion in what is quoted.

Ideally, any attempt to construct a rounded and honest account of the whole curriculum (which as David Hamilton 1990 points out, is always to some extent 'an unfinished curriculum') would seek to balance evidence gathered through interview against the kinds of evidence reviewed in the previous two chapters; classroom observation, for example, or examination results as a measure of pupil achievement. Seen in this light, 'triangulation' is not (as is sometimes suggested) simply a means of checking the insights derived from one kind of evidence against the insights derived from another. Rather, it is an acknowledgement that these different data gathering methods represent different, and complementary, ways of seeing. What we learn from a review of pupil attendance can usefully be juxtaposed against what we learn from, say, a round of pupil interviews. But the one can never cancel the other out or render its insights redundant.

Louis Cohen and Lawrence Manion (1980: 211) suggest that the use of multiple methods is in fact, however, only one type of triangulation. Their typology of triangulation (based on Denzin 1970) includes, in addition to methodological triangulation, five categories:

- time triangulation (using cross-sectional and longitudinal designs);
- space triangulation (extending across sites and/or cultures);
- combined levels of triangulation (drawing on evidence from individuals, groups and collectivities);
- theoretical triangulation (using alternative or competing theories in preference to one viewpoint only); and
- investigator triangulation (engaging more than one observer).

Given the possibility of building into their designs these kinds of checks and balances, evaluators should be in a position to claim a fair measure of intellectual rigour for their work. Certainly, the claim by Janet Powney and Mike Watts (1987: 193) that, as far as interviewing in educational research is concerned, 'the choice between lie or story . . . depends on what the reader wants to know, what respondents do or what respondents would like to think they do' should be read as an admission of sloppiness rather than as a serious methodological statement. For any interviewer who thinks carefully about the overall design of the evaluation and about the detailed analysis of the interview evidence that has been gathered, it is simply untrue that (as Powney and Watts (1987) suggest) 'the best an interviewer can hope for is insight into the respondent's favourite self-image'. He or she can, and should, hope for a great deal more.

Summary

A recurring theme throughout this and the previous two chapters has been the need for an eclectic approach which brings together qualitative and quantitative methods and values the insights to be derived from each. In considering the processes and procedures whereby that evidence, once collected, can be shared and made public, we shall, in the following chapter, be placing a continuing emphasis on the need for an eclectic and flexible system of evaluation; a system, that is, which fulfils the diverse needs of different groups and audiences, including the staff development needs of teachers in schools.

– 7 –

The Knowable Community

The last three chapters have been concerned with methods and sources of data collection and analysis. This chapter looks at how, once gathered and sifted, evaluation evidence might be presented to colleagues and others and how, through discussion, this might itself lead to further analysis and clarification. That process of discussion – of working through, and on, the issues as they emerge, so as to define them more sharply – is never easy. It amounts, after all, to an attempt on behalf of schools to know themselves: to become more knowing and, indeed, more knowable communities.

That phrase – the knowable community – is Raymond Williams's and he is writing about the English novel. He argues that the development of the novel from Dickens to Lawrence should be seen in relation to 'the very rapidly increasing size and scale and complexity of communities' during the period of that development. Within that changing context 'any assumption of a knowable community – a whole community, wholly knowable – becomes harder and harder to sustain' (Williams 1970: 17). It is 'a term used with irony because what is known is shown to be incomplete' (Williams 1979: 171). The problem to which the novel might be seen as a response, therefore, is how we can make that complexity habitable. How can we render it knowable?

Evaluation, conceived as something other than a mere curriculum audit or an exercise in appraisal, might be seen as the response to a very similar kind of problem. For it is not only the community within which schools are located that has become 'unknowable in terms of manifest experience' (Williams 1979: 247), but the policy framework within which schools have to operate and, indeed, the organization and ethos of schools themselves. Under these circumstances it is important to bear in mind that 'what is knowable is not only a function of objects – of what is there to be known. It is also a function of subjects, of observers – what is desired and what needs to be known.' A knowable community, in other words, 'is a matter of consciousness as well as of evident fact' (Williams 1970: 17).

The culture of teaching

What is all too often seen simply as a technical problem to do with report writing or whatever is also, then, a cultural problem to do with the sense that teachers, parents, pupils and others make of schooling. 'The urgent need', as John Sayer (1989: 13) points out, 'is not just for schools to be managed more effectively, but for society, including its teachers, to capture some common sense of what effect it wishes schools to have.' How can evaluation help to articulate and communicate that 'common sense'? How can it enable schools, in all their changing complexity, to become knowable communities?

These questions are a far cry from the terms usually employed to discuss the process of dissemination and reporting. Jean Rudduck (1976: 7) usefully highlighted a significant shift in emphasis in the mid-1970s whereby 'diffusion' became a more directed, deliberate and 'centrally managed process of dissemination, training, and the provision of resources and incentives'. Those involved in curriculum research and development confirmed they 'meant business by hauling down the modest pennant of diffusion and marching under new colours – the bold banner of dissemination' (Rudduck 1986a: 108). In doing so, however (as Rudduck herself argues), they discarded more than they realized at the time: the idea, for example, of 'dissemination' as an 'encounter of cultures' (Rudduck, 1978) that is framed by 'the dominant structures and values that hold habit in place' (Rudduck 1986b: 7).

Those structures and values may, at some level, be tenaciously and (as Rudduck suggests) 'properly' conservative. There need to be lines of continuity. Indeed, schools rely upon those continuities to ensure that they 'are not easily thrown into disarray by curricular fads and fancies, whimsical novelties and light persuasions'. The reverse side of that coin, however, is that schools may become 'equally impervious to what we think of as our reasoned, relevant and legitimate proposals for curriculum change' (Rudduck 1986b: 9). The culture of teaching cuts both ways.

The more negative aspects of that culture are caught somewhat unkindly (though the central tenets of his argument are kindly enough) by David Hargreaves (1982: 200–1) in a vignette which perhaps owes more to fictional stereotype than empirical observation:

> The English schoolmaster is soon recognised on a hot summer day in the Vatican museums, not merely by his Harris-tweed jacket, but by the fact that, armed with his guidebook of authoritative knowledge, he will be haranguing his spouse and children just as if they were 3B out on a school visit. The thirst for knowledge is admirable; the determination to pass it on verbally less so. It breeds a constant and obsessive desire to be expert, to be omniscient.

The caricature conjured up by Hargreaves does highlight one of the problems inherent in the culture of teaching: its emphasis on the teacher as the one who knows best, together with all the stresses and frustrations that this misguided notion drags in its wake. There are, however, other, very different strains inherent in that same culture: its emphasis on mutual support; its insistence on care as a key factor in learning; and, above all, its assumption that the school is central to the life of the local community. What characterizes these more positive aspects is not, as David Hargreaves (1982: 93) surmises, 'the fallacy of individualism', but rather a predilection for 'mucking in': for conceiving of, and following through, a joint task and enjoying oneself in the process.

Any approach to evaluation must, of course, acknowledge the blockage represented by the teacher as the one who knows best mentality, but a collegial approach to evaluation must, in addition, connect with the existing traditions of collaboration and mutual support among teachers. Alan O'Connor (1989: 70) adds a useful gloss on the notion of the knowable community when he suggests that it 'implies a contrast with one that is already known'. To envisage the school as a knowable community is to build upon the collegial aspects of teaching in order to achieve a different, and as yet still emergent, culture of schooling; one based, that is, upon reflective practice and shared understanding.

The process of sharing the evidence derived from evaluation (whether or not this takes the form of a written report) is, then, a highly complex cultural intervention. It is not enough simply to throw wise words at one's colleagues. One needs to create a space in which the evidence is reviewed and discussed and its implications considered for the various individuals and groups concerned. 'Findings' are not inert facts presenting themselves to the passive and disinterested observer; they are what we discover – by way of insight and significance – in the process of engaging with the evidence. What is 'found' is, to return to Williams, in part at least a function of what we as subjects, as observers, need and want to know. Evaluation must create its own climate of curiosity – its own common sense of what needs to be known – if its insights are to illuminate the policy and practice of schooling.

Occasions and continua

So we return again to the notions of professionalism and collegiality. For without these any attempt at evaluation becomes either marginalized ('What a good idea – if only there were time!') or rebuffed ('Evaluation? That's a kind of inspection isn't it?'). But once linked to the idea of professed values – their articulation, their translation into practice, the possibility of their loss – evaluation comes very close to the heart of whatever it means to be a teacher. To be effective a collegial approach to evaluation must relate closely to the aims and overall programme of professional development and in-service education within the school.

Before discussing in more detail the production of written evaluation reports, we shall therefore look at some of the contexts within which evaluation might relate to such a programme and thereby fulfil an important INSET function. What follows is, in many ways, little more than an annotated list of ideas and, as such, is by no means exhaustive. Each of the forums listed below does, however, offer an opportunity for evaluation to become a prime focus for the sharing of insights and information, ideas and practices, problems and possibilities; a focus, that is, for the continuing professional development of teachers and the enriching of the school's culture and ethos.

Staff meetings

Learning, as Lawrence Stenhouse (1981) once reminded a gathering of drama teachers, is an occasion as well as a continuum. One of the problems with the professional development of teachers, however, is that it tends to be all continuum and very little occasion. The routine meetings that might provide an occasion for real learning – department meetings, faculty meetings, house meetings, year meetings, full staff meetings, and the like – are pulled along in the slipstream of planning and implementation, decision making and development. Evaluation is at best the last item on an overcrowded agenda.

This is a pity, since such meetings offer an ideal opportunity for reporting evaluation findings and discussing their implications; an opportunity, that is, to stop, think and question. The structure of meetings in any school has to deal with a lot of business, but clearings can – and should – be made for other, more reflective kinds of discussion: occasions when the exploration of differing and possibly divergent viewpoints around key issues and questions is (and is acknowledged to be) more important than the achievement of a consensus around agreed outcomes.

Occasional workshops

INSET days, too, can provide an opportunity for groups of teachers to share evaluation evidence and to analyse it with a view to gaining fresh insights into their own classroom practice. One group, for example, might listen to, and discuss, a tape recording of a small-group discussion among pupils; another group might discuss the classroom observation notes produced as part of an exercise in collaborative teaching; while a third group might review the range of work produced across subject areas by certain pupils within a particular time span: see Nixon and Watts 1989.

Where groups of teachers have already begun to sift and shape the evidence they have gathered, more formal presentations might be used as a starting point for discussion. These could take the form of a brief case study of a particular lesson or course of lessons, using a range of evidence (for example, pupil feedback, notes made by an outside observer, interviews with the teachers involved) to highlight issues and concerns for consideration by the staff as a whole. Alternatively, a group could choose to present a brief summary paper outlining some of the insights they have derived from evaluating their own work.

Seminars with invited outsiders

On certain occasions it might be useful to invite specialists in from outside the school to help analyse the evidence gathered. If, for example, a group of teachers has been looking at patterns of attendance and truancy within the school, it might be helpful for those teachers to discuss their findings with a number of invited outsiders: someone, for example, who is conversant with the relevant research literature in this field; someone who has informed views on the factors affecting truancy generally and the particular factors pertaining within the school; and someone who is experienced in processing and analysing this kind of evidence and who might therefore point out unforeseen pitfalls and further lines of enquiry.

One of the problems with specialists is that they tend to like the sound of their own voices. It is important to ensure, therefore, that those attending understand the purpose of the seminar: they are there to listen to, and assist, the teachers who are carrying out the evaluation, not simply to sound off on their pet theories. They are more likely to fulfil this function if they are sent relevant papers in advance, together with a list of questions and themes that are to be explored. In the past the LEA advisory service would have been an obvious source of expertise to draw on. However, given the changing role of the advisory service, schools might also wish to draw on other sources. Over time a school might well develop an extensive list of contacts that it can call on in this way.

Exhibitions and displays

Some kinds of evaluation evidence may lend themselves to visual display; in the staffroom, say, or in a room used for regular staff gatherings. If the display is situated in a more public position where pupils and visitors have access to it, care should be taken to ensure that it is neither too critical and negative nor purely celebratory. To serve an evaluative purpose, a display or exhibition of this kind must be arranged in such a way as to draw people in and invite them to ask questions and think about the evidence being presented. It should stimulate curiosity and discussion and for that very reason should be neither threatening nor cosy.

One of the problems with displays is that it is all too easy to pass them by with little more than a cursory glance. They are most effective when mounted for a limited and specified period of time and when linked to relevant events. A survey of curriculum choices at 14 + highlighting issues of gender and questions relating to future career routes might, for example, be a useful accompaniment to a third-year parents' evening. Similarly, the period set aside for work experience might be an ideal time to display any available evauation evidence on previous work experience placements. In terms of dissemination, the impact of any visual display is likely to be limited; as a means of reinforcing the notion of the school as a knowable, enquiring community, its impact can, however, be considerable.

Conferences

In certain instances a school may feel that it wishes to share its findings with other schools involved in evaluating their own practice, with other research institutions and with other individuals and groups within the education service. Under these circumstances it may be possible to organize, perhaps in conjunction with neighbouring schools, a conference in which a number of institutions present their findings and discuss these with one another.

Research conferences are not usually initiated and organized by schools. If, however, we are to take seriously the idea of schools as being central to the educational research community, then there is no reason why schools should not use such gatherings as occasions for presenting their evaluation evidence to a wider audience. Funding could, of course, present a very real problem, but provided the event were comparatively small scale and the financial burden spread across institutions this need not be insurmountable: see Nixon, Magee and Sheard (1979) for a report of such a conference.

None of the occasions highlighted above are likely to have much lasting impact if they are seen as one off events. Learning, to turn Stenhouse's dichotomy on its head, is not just an occasion: it is also a continuum. And a continuum is more than just a sequence of unrelated occurrences: it is, to quote the definition offered in the *Oxford English Dictionary*, a 'thing of continuous structure'. If evaluation is to be taken seriously as a means of helping teachers to go on learning about their own teaching, it must therefore relate directly and explicitly to the on going programme of professional development within the school.

The concept of audience

It will be obvious from the previous examples that the written report is only one of several ways in which evaluation findings can be presented so as to inform discussions both within the school and between the school and the wider community. Nevertheless, the written report remains a significant and influential means of presentation, not only because it has a permanence which is denied to, say, the verbal report or the visual display, but because it is able to reach a potentially much wider audience. It creates a readership: a diaspora of historically and geographically distanced individuals all focusing upon a common text.

So what considerations need to be taken into account in preparing such a report? What form should a written report take? What should it include and leave out? Where should schools start in compiling and structuring evaluation reports relating to their own policy and practice?

As Robert McCormick and Mary James (1983: 295) point out, 'a key to the form of any report is the concept of audience'. They distinguish four main audience groups (parents, governors, the education committee of the local authority, and other professionals) and raise an important question regarding a fifth group:

> what of pupils as an audience? . . . If teachers argue that researchers and outside evaluators ignore their needs and concerns when investigating them, pupils can make the same complaint when teachers evaluate the schools and classrooms in which they spend twenty-five hours a week.
>
> (McCormick and James 1983: 304)

Schools will have no difficulty in adding to this list. For example, local employers may on occasion be an appropriate audience, while any external agencies that contribute funds or resources to the school may also require some form of written evaluation. It may well be that more than one audience group is involved, in which case those responsible for conducting the evaluation will have to decide whether a single report will suffice or whether the needs of each group is sufficiently distinct to call for separate reports.

The purpose of the report

Different audiences imply different purposes and this, too, is an important determinant of the form of any written report. Where, for example, the purpose is to inform the senior management team regarding a choice to be made between a limited number of pre-specified options, a fairly brief summary report outlining the perceived advantages and disadvantages of each option may be appropriate. A fuller report, giving the reader a stronger flavour of the evidence that has been gathered, may on the other hand be more appropriate where the purpose is to raise the awareness of other professionals, and possibly parents, regarding, say, the value of a recent curriculum initiative.

What is important is that, as the author of such a document, one starts by asking whom one is addressing and why; and by acknowledging that writing is primarily a process of selection (one cannot tell all). The rest – what is included and left out, the level of generality, the formality of tone – all follows from that. The best in this kind are, after all, but 'systems, or economies, of truth' (Clifford 1986: 7).

So when Marvin Alkin (1987: 323) writes that 'the evaluation report must be in language understandable to the decision-maker', he is in fact writing about a particular kind of evaluation report: one addressed, that is, to 'the decision-maker'. Such a report might well prove incomprehensible, simplistic, or just plain boring to other kinds of audience that may be looking to evaluation to fulfil different kinds of purposes: the parent, for example, who is trying to understand more about how the school operates, or a group of teachers in a neighbouring school who want to get a feel for a particular teaching style.

In such cases, where there is a less direct relation between the report and the decision-maker, narrative may prove a useful form of presentation. The great strength of the story form is that it refuses to take for granted the linearity of cause and effect. Stories very rarely say, 'Because this happened, that happened'. They keep their options open. 'This happened and then that happened' is more their style. In trying to convey something of the complexity of classroom life, narrative's implicit acknowledgement of causal indeterminacy, of the sheer contingency of social reality, can be a distinct advantage. It lets readers in on the evaluative act by inviting them to interpret events for themselves, to reflect upon what happened and why, and to speculate about possible futures.

Where a report is intended to inform particular policy choices, the narrative form is likely to be less appropriate. The decision making group will almost certainly be working to a tight schedule and its members will require the report to have done some of their thinking for them. Such a report is likely, therefore, to be more analytical, outlining the options open and possibly making recommendations on the basis of the evidence gathered. It will also need to be brief and concise, so as to provide a clear focus for discussion at whatever meeting it is being formally presented.

Report timeliness

The timeliness of such a report is one of its most vital attributes. As Malvin Alkin (1987: 325) again puts it, 'an evaluation must provide the information that a decision-maker needs before the decision is made'. This may sound like stating the obvious, but can present a number of problems. For a start, an educational evaluator tends to think in terms of the school year, while a decision maker may well be thinking in terms of a budget making cycle that comes full circle at the end of the financial year. Or, to take a related problem, neither the evaluators nor the decision makers may have taken sufficient reckoning of the time taken to clear the evidence presented in the report.

Both these problems arise from inadequate prior consultation between those who are conducting the evaluation and those to whom their report is addressed. They are perhaps more likely to occur when the audience being addressed is external to the school; but given the very different roles and responsibilities of groups and individuals within medium to large schools, such problems can also affect the internal reporting of evaluation results. It is important to ensure, therefore, that when the purpose of the evaluation is to inform a particular set of decisions, the evaluation schedule should be planned back from the point at which those decisions have to be made and should leave ample time for clearance of evidence, for rewriting and for the preparation of the final draft.

Pupils as audience

But what, to return to that earlier question, of pupils as an audience? How do they figure in all this? When we think of the decision maker, we tend to have an image of someone located in what is euphemistically referred to as a position of responsibility but might be more accurately designated a position of power: an adult, certainly; usually male; and invariably white. Against this powerful image need to be posed many others: images of those who, though without power, still have difficult decisions to make. Among these other images are our pupils.

Little work (as far as I know) has been done on the involvement of pupils, either in the earlier stages of the evaluation process or as a possible audience for evaluation reports. Some related and relevant work has been undertaken, however, on the problems inherent in the introduction of pupils to innovative teaching styles and learning experiences. Jean Rudduck (1991: 66), drawing on her experience of the Humanities Curriculum Project, argues a strong case for the use of videotape as a means of introducing pupils to new ways of thinking and working:

> First, it legitimizes the involvement of pupils and teachers in innovation. They see other groups, in recognizable school settings, behaving in the 'abnormal' way of the innovation. In their often conventional climates of schools, this can be helpful . . . Secondly, videotape provides a shared image of the 'strange' behaviour of the innovation that can be analysed by the group, and out of this analysis the group may come to build their own sense of form.

Rudduck spells out the more general point that lies behind this example as follows:

> the principles of an innovation are best communicated through a shared experience of the principles in action, and if this cannot be achieved within the group itself, then it may be attempted through a surrogate experience of the principles in action that videotape can supply.

For the purposes of the present argument the example offered by Rudduck, and the general point that underlies it, is important on two other counts. It reminds us that the written report is not always the most appropriate form of presentation and that, regardless of the form adopted, the context within which the report is presented contributes greatly to its impact. No report, whether written or otherwise, can make a lasting impact, or even superficial impression, if it is cast to the wind. A culture must be there to nurture and sustain it.

External reports

A rigid distinction between internal and external reporting is difficult to maintain. This is partly because any piece of writing, once produced, tends to have a life of its own (an evaluation report originally intended for internal consumption may reach a much wider audience as a result of subsequent release); and partly because some groups and individuals are both 'insiders' and 'outsiders', depending upon the particular function they are fulfilling at any one time (governors, LEA advisers and parents, for example, all have this ambiguity attached to their role).

Nevertheless, there are occasions when evaluation reports are addressed primarily, and explicitly, to groups acting in a contractual accountability relation to the school. Such groups, fulfilling that kind of accountability function, might be said to be unambiguously 'external' and can as an audience, therefore, present a somewhat threatening prospect. It is at this junction, for example, that the LEA adviser crosses some invisible boundary whereby he or she is translated into an 'inspector'; or the governors who have taken such trouble to become a part of the school community have to realize their legal responsibility to represent other, broader constituencies.

It is all too easy for schools to become obsessed with the credibility of the reports they address to such audiences. Credibility is, of course, an important factor, but, as McCormick and James (1983: 297–8) rightly point out, 'credibility is not just a matter of methodological soundness or veracity of the reports'. It depends also upon the prejudices and predilections of the readers, who may, for example, 'have a naive confidence in the rigour of any study which uses quantitative measures and a suspicion of qualitative data – irrespective of the thoroughness with which an evaluation is conducted'.

A collegial approach to evaluation has an important role to play in all this: by raising awareness among the potential readership as to the purposes and procedures of educational evaluation and, as a consequence of this, helping to create a context in which different kinds of evaluation reports can be sensitively received and promptly acted upon. Clearly, the predispositions of the reader cannot be ignored, but they can, and ought, to be given an occasional nudge. Certainly, any evaluation report addressed to such an audience should spell out the aims of the evaluation and include a brief section outlining the procedures adopted and sources of evidence drawn on.

It should also explain, clearly and briefly, the relevance of these, if there is any possibility of misunderstanding.

External audiences are likely to need reminding also of the resource implications of any evaluation exercise. If, for example, fifteen days have been earmarked for evaluation, it should be understood from the outset that this includes time for preparation, data gathering, analysis and writing up. Five days spent on the latter means that there is that much less time for gathering evidence and processing it. A longer, supposedly more detailed report may mean that there is in fact less detailed evidence to draw on; whereas a brief summary report may actually be based on richer and more varied evidence (simply because more time has been set aside to gather it).

The important general point to bear in mind is that external audiences require careful handling. The golden rule is never to take them by surprise. Keep them informed and, wherever possible, reach a formal agreement with them regarding key aspects of the evaluation. This can help to avoid later tensions. If, for example, the time scale of the evaluation, the extent of the evidence gathered, and the major themes to be addressed are all agreed along the way, the final report can be less easily rejected out of hand.

Nevertheless, it is all too easy for an external audience, having commissioned or requested an evaluation report, to disregard its findings. In my (by now, fairly long) experience of producing such reports, I have come across three common responses. These, in descending order of subtlety, I categorize as *shelving*, *sidestepping* and *rubbishing*.

The first is the most common. It involves the formal acceptance of the report (with perhaps some minor modifications), a sentence or two of gratitude for those who have produced it, even some positive mutterings regarding the significance of its findings. And then: nothing. The report is literally *shelved* and only referred to again in order to prove that some evaluation has actually taken place.

An alternative response is for the audience to *sidestep* the report by arguing that its agreed focus is now somehow less relevant than it was at the outset. Events are said, or more usually just thought, to have overtaken the enquiry. No one, so the argument goes, is to blame for this: it is just that the evaluation has become something of an academic exercise: useful for all that; but not quite so relevant as everyone had hoped. Even when, throughout and prior to the evaluation, those carrying it out have liaised as fully as possible with their audience, this kind of defensive ploy is not uncommon, particularly within the current context, in which externally enforced change can be seen radically to alter the agenda of issues and concerns addressed by a school.

Rubbishing can take one of several forms. The most common of these is to import a concept from one research paradigm and insinuate it into one with very different traditions and validating procedures: as when, for example, the detailed study of a single case is dismissed on the grounds that it falls short of the minimum sample size. Another ploy is to deflect attention away from the report and on to its authors: by suggesting, for example, that any evaluation conducted by teachers into their own classroom practice will necessarily be subjective and uncritical. Such criticisms can be devastating, precisely because they are based on such false assumptions. It is, after all, very difficult to reason against the ignorance of those to whom one is contractually accountable, without appearing either defensive or aggressive.

These kinds of problems can, as already suggested, be largely overcome by evaluators taking the trouble to consult with their audience before and during the evaluation period. The responsibility, however, does not lie entirely with those who produce the evaluation report. The reader, too, shares responsibility for making the evaluation work; for ensuring, that is, that the insights the report generates are recognized and, where appropriate, acted upon. This, to be sure, is no easy matter. Any evaluation which takes seriously the task of rendering the school more knowable is unlikely to fall conveniently into a single methodological category. It will need to focus both on ethnographic-type detail and on other, more abstract processes that can only be grasped statistically or analytically. The ideal evaluation report is likely, therefore, to be something of a 'combinatory text' and its ideal reader someone who understands that neither ethnography (with its 'deep synchronic bias') nor statistical analysis (with its habit 'of fixing the states of society and culture as already formed') is on its own enough (Marcus and Fischer 1986: 77–110).

Summary

To return to the central theme of this chapter: the evaluation report is only one of the ways in which the insights derived from evaluation can be brought to bear on policy and practice and the written report only one of several forms such a report may take. Any attempt to evaluate, even when those conducting the evaluation are part of what is being evaluated, is potentially threatening and disruptive. Only within a trusting and sympathetic context, in which participants have neither forgotten how to be curious nor are afraid to ask questions, can evaluation become a means of self-knowledge. Such contexts do not come ready made. They have to be constructed, sometimes at the expense of much time and effort. But it is an essential task, for, without it, evaluation can have no hope of being collegial in either its procedures or its outcomes.

– 8 –

Beyond the Secret Garden

The purpose of this final chapter is to gather the major themes of the book and relate them to some of the broader management issues that schools will have to face in finding ways to sustain and support reflective practice among teachers. We start as always with questions – a lot of them – but also with some serious reservations about the National Curriculum and the policy framework within which it is developing. Thanks to the 1988 Education Reform Act, the school curriculum has been well and truly removed from its secret garden and is now very much in the public domain. A major managerial task for the future, therefore, will be to ensure that, in making that move, schools go on being places where teachers can think about their own teaching and about what it means to learn.

More questions than answers

There is a growing sense that within the UK the National Curriculum now constitutes the parameters of the debate on curriculum; that, as David McNamara (1990: 226) puts it, 'there is little point in continuing to challenge the philosophical and educational basis of the national curriculum (in so far as these exist)'. From this perspective the traditions and practices of curriculum development and evaluation are circumscribed by the first chapter of the first part of the 1988 Education Reform Act. Even those who (like David McNamara above) have reservations, offer these in the form of a negative, resigned support for what is acknowledged (in parentheses) to be wrong-headed (i.e. having little or no 'philosophical and educational basis'). This is undoubtedly a recipe for despair: to be constructing our agendas around a notion of curriculum to which, as educationists, we have deeply ambivalent responses.

That ambivalence, however, cuts deep. Some fifteen years ago (Thursday 14 October 1976, to be exact) the then Secretary of State for Industry recorded in his personal diary the following comment:

> Cabinet at 10. I asked Shirley about the reports that Jim is going to make a major education speech and she passed me a note saying, 'Tony, no question of any change in emphasis on comprehensives. It's mainly on maths, why not enough kids are doing engineering, etc. A bit about standards. Curriculum will be the main row.'
>
> (Benn 1989: 626)

The main row

Curriculum is still, of course, the main row. But, like most rows, it has a history. This particular row reaches back beyond Thatcherism, beyond even the Great Debate and its aftermath (see CCCS 1981: 208–27). It has its roots in the ideal of comprehensivization and the need to work through the curriculum and pedagogical implications of that ideal.

As early as 1961, Raymond Williams was heading us in this direction when, in *The Long Revolution*, he attempted to define 'the minimum to aim at for every educationally normal child'. It is interesting, thirty years on, to glance back at Williams's (1965: 174–5) version of a national, 'common' curriculum:

- extensive practice in the fundamental languages of English and mathematics;
- general knowledge of ourselves and our environment, taught at the secondary stage not as separate academic disciplines but as general knowledge drawn from the disciplines which clarify at a higher stage . . .;
- history and criticism of literature, the visual arts, music, dramatic performance, landscape and architecture;
- extensive practice in democratic procedures, including meetings, negotiations, and the selection and conduct of leaders in

democratic organisations . . . [and] in the use of libraries, news-
papers and magazines, radio and television programmes, and
other sources of information, opinion and influence;

- introduction to at least one other culture, including its language,
history, geography, institutions and arts, to be given in part by
visiting and exchange.

It is all there: the core, foundation and cross-curriculum elements;
balanced science; and, by implication, citizenship. There is nothing
new under the sun; which is perhaps one of the reasons (there are, of
course, others) why opposition to the 1988 version, though spirited,
has been at best sporadic. The idea of some kind of national curriculum connects only too well with the urge towards a common curriculum that has been at the forefront of educational debate for the
last quarter of a century. The National Curriculum as it is shaping
up under the auspices of the NCC may be a poor parody of an older,
more egalitarian idea, but parodies (even poor ones) present a difficult target.

Particularly so when, as in this case, they are able to exploit a
centuries old semantic tension implicit in the word 'common'. For
that word may be used to denote something shared or to describe
something ordinary; something 'low' and 'vulgar'. There are considerable and persistent overlaps in these uses and Williams (1976: 61)
again points up the difficulty of disentangling them historically:

> In feudal society the (negative) attribution was systematic and
> carried few if any additional overtones. It is significant that
> members of the Parliamentary army in the Civil War . . .
> refused to be called 'common soldiers' and insisted on 'private
> soldiers'. This must indicate an existing and derogatory sense
> of 'common', though it is interesting that this same army were
> fighting for 'the commons' and went on to establish a 'com-
> monwealth'. The alternative they chose is remarkable, since it
> asserted, in the true spirit of their revolution, that they were
> their own men.

The row rumbles on. Is the National Curriculum really about
people becoming their own persons? Or is it (in defensive recoil,
perhaps, from that derogatory sense of 'common') about the 'pri-
vatization' of education? Does it indicate social division or social
cohesion: 'a whole group or interest or a large specific and subordinate group'? (Williams 1976: 61) What does the National Curricu-

lum really mean for the teachers who have to implement it and the pupils who will have to pass through it?

The policy framework

In approaching these questions we need to remind ourselves that the National Curriculum is part of a legislative package which not only 'represents the biggest quantum leap in direct control over detailed pedagogy and classroom activity ever undertaken' (Fletcher 1990: 68), but also aims at radically changing the ethos and culture of schooling. The Education Reform Act of 1988 is, as Stephen Bates (1990) points out, 'an uneasy amalgam of interventionist regulation (464 additional powers for the Secretary of State) and free market rhetoric'. The introduction of the National Curriculum and testing at 7, 11, 14 and 16 must be set against the revised arrangements for the admission of pupils to state schools (ERA, Part 1, Chapter 2), the system of delegated school budgets (Chapter 3), the procedures to enable schools to opt out of LEA control (Chapter 4), the establishment of 'city technology colleges' (Chapter 5) and the abolition of the ILEA (Part 3).

The inconsistency inherent in this package is neatly summed up by John Sayer (1989: 55):

> There appears to be a view in government which is alternatively centralistic and anarchic: central government will determine in detail what should be taught and examined in schools in the public service; but every encouragement should be given for either schools or individual parents to opt out of that service, and to exercise collective and individual parental choice even if that disrupts the planning of educational provision for the local community, or is socially divisive.

The long-term effect of the changed policy framework within which the National Curriculum is now set is difficult to gauge. It will, however, undoubtedly increase the inequalities between schools. It will also, in spite of resistance by many teachers and headteachers, create a competitive climate in which corporate planning across schools will become much more difficult. This lack of regional planning is already having an impact on the provision of in-service education and training. With LEA advisory services being pulled towards an inspectorial role and the logistics of teacher secondment becoming that much more complex, the traditional patterns of inservice provision are being put under increased pressure (Stillman and Grant 1989.)

'Any serious attempt to establish a collegial approach to evaluation over the next few years will have to relate to these broader policy developments and, in so doing, hold open the option of 'continuing to challenge the philosophical and educational basis of the National Curriculum (in so far as these exist)'. If those working in schools are to understand what is happening in and across their institutions, they will need to address a broad range of policy issues and to insist on the relevance of those issues to the task of effective management. That insistence, moreover, is likely to become increasingly difficult to maintain as the role of curriculum evaluation becomes associated with, if not reduced to, monitoring the cumulative data drawn from successive waves of SATs.

Schools will need, then, to address some basic questions about the ways in which the policy framework established by ERA is influencing the work of schools. How, for example, is 'open enrolment' affecting their ethos and culture? What effect is opting out – or the possibility of it – having on collegial relationships and supportive networks across schools? What is LMS doing to roles and designated responsibilities within particular institutions? What is happening to the curriculum of those schools that are losing potential pupils to the newly established city technology colleges?

Managing the middle ground

The task, as Nicholas Beattie (1990: 39) defines it,

> is now to create a new 'culture of education' in which curriculum is better supported and understood by the community. What that culture will look like is difficult to predict, but it will certainly . . . require the forging of new alliances between educational professionals and other groups, a redefinition of teacher roles and professional autonomy, a greater willingness to communicate and negotiate.

The nature of these 'new alliances' will be an important factor effecting the involvement of schools in the evaluation of their own practice. Any group of teachers adopting a collegial approach to evaluation will eventually want, and need, to think through its findings with other teachers including those from neighbouring schools and colleges. In the past there have been mechanisms – teachers' centres, teacher secondments, LEA in-service sessions – whereby this kind of cross-institutional sharing and corporate planning has been at the very least a possibility in almost all areas. Now, many of those mechanisms are at risk.

A role for the LEA?

LEAs, which traditionally provided that kind of regional planning and overview, are under particularly severe threat. One strand of central government thinking has been that LEAs constitute a kind of mezzanine that only serves to overload the system as a whole and thereby render it less efficient. Would it not be easier just to do away with LEAs altogether and have schools funded directly by, and accountable directly to, central government? Could not the kind of consortia that have been developed, to sometimes good effect, under the TVEI extension scheme fulfil the functions of the LEA? Who, in short, needs an LEA?

Margaret Maden (1990) challenges that particular line of thought, on the grounds not only that it ignores 'the importance of links between education and social services, physical and economic planning systems and sports, parks, museums and libraries', but also that it fails to make sense in terms of the internal management of the education service. In short, it is just plain silly. That silliness, she points out, is highlighted if we consider how a consortium would decide whether or not a new school needed to be built:

> Presumably the consortium would need something approximating to a local authority near at hand so that longer term demographic and housing developments could be established before reaching their decision? The consortium would then, one assumes, negotiate with neighbouring consortia on the realisation of capital assets and manage the borrowing requirements and debt repayments needed for such a capital scheme to proceed? At this point, I would think the consortium would be begging for an LEA to be reinvented.

It would be an error to assume, therefore, that the abolition of LEAs necessarily follows from the devolution of financial responsibility to schools: 'this is the error of the abolitionists' (Bill Dennison 1990). 'They risk the bureaucracy of a centralised system because they overlook what schools cannot and should not be made to do.' Dennison goes on to highlight four main functions which schools 'should not be made to do' and which, taken together, define for LEAs a continuing and 'indispensable role': *strategy* ('deciding the number of schools, their location, size, and age range'); *monitoring* ('the curriculum, standards of teaching and quality of accommodation'); *arbitration* ('between parents and a school over a disciplinary matter, when a teacher has an employment grievance, where a school's admission's policy is contested, and so on'); and *services* ('meals, curriculum advice, salary payments, structural repairs, and so on').

This insistence on the continuing role of the LEA is not to deny the importance of schools grouping together to share and to plan beyond the immediate needs of the individual school. After all, as Margaret Maden (1990) acknowledges, such groupings 'provide a practical structure within which constructive links and mutual dependencies could be realised'. Whether or not they will be realized must depend, however, on whether LEAs are allowed to continue in a supportive role; and that, in turn, will depend in some measure on the determination of schools to use every facility available to ensure that those 'constructive links and mutual dependencies' are strengthened and extended.

Thus, although the power base of schooling has shifted significantly away from LEAs, their still considerable influence on local and regional planning and the development of an effective evaluation and staff development programme is of immense and continuing value. Neil Fletcher (1990: 70) reinforces the earlier point made by Margaret Maden when he argues that, 'if LEAs had not already existed, . . . Kenneth Baker would have had to invent them in order to provide a credible means of implementing his reforms'. The question remains, however, as to whether Baker's successors at the DES will appreciate this point and, if so, how schools can, and should, respond to what will anyway be very much a 'new alliance'.

Interdependent professionals

Central to such an alliance will be a shared understanding between schools and LEAs as to the nature and purpose of evaluation. The responsibilities laid upon LEAs to secure the implementation of the National Curriculum will, as the Audit Commission's (1989: 17) report on the role of LEA inspectors and advisers pointed out, require 'the development of more systematic monitoring, with more intensive direct observation of teaching and learning and better record-keeping'. A recent survey conducted by David Nebesnuick (1990: 8) suggested that there are three main paths an LEA can take in order to fulfil these responsibilities: 'it can rely very heavily upon self-evaluation methods within the schools or it can adopt an external inspection system or quite possibly it can pursue a combination of the two'.

Based upon the evidence of fifty LEAs, the survey found that twenty-five of these inclined towards a system which emphasized the importance of 'local internal mechanisms'. Moreover, several of these LEAs 'referred to the need for individual schools to develop school-based performance indicators relevant to their local needs and circumstances', rather than being dependent upon 'comprehensive authority-wide indicators' (Nebesnuick 1990: 6–7). Although the evidence of the survey suggests that the 'local internal mechanisms' that are being established vary considerably across authorities, it presents a far from depressing prospect of the way in which in-school evaluation procedures might become a significant element within authority-wide systems of evaluation.

Brian Wilcox, through the work of his Inspection Methodologies for Education and Training (IMET) project, also sees institutional self-evaluation as a necessary activity in any effective authority-wide evaluation programme (see Wilcox 1991a and 1991b). It is, he argues, one of several inter-related component activities, which would include (1989):

- the development and use of performance indicators;
- inspection;
- systematic visits by advisers;
- institutional self-evaluation;
- specialist evaluation.

It would be a mistake, however, to view the development of such systems simply as a bureaucratic exercise. If teachers are to aspire to what Peter Ribbins (1990: 91) has termed 'interdependent professionalism', they will need to ensure that whatever system is developed is consistent with their own professed values; that it is, in other words, a system of educational evaluation, rather than an evaluation system that is grafted on to their own educational practices. While educational evaluation may be subsidiarily concerned with questions of efficiency, cost effectiveness and value for money (the shibboleths of current orthodoxy), its prime concern must be to focus upon the education process itself. Insofar as evaluation is value driven, its values must be the professed values of the educator. A key concern, therefore, for all those involved in the evaluation of schools must be to define its distinguishing features; to make explicit, in other words, what it is that is educational about educational evaluation.

As 'interdependent professionals' teachers will need to address this concern in partnership with a wide range of professional groups. Earlier chapters have emphasized, for example, the valuable support that colleagues working in institutions of higher education can offer in terms of consultancy, classroom observation and interviewing. As Jean Rudduck (1991: 141) points out, 'schools and universities need to plan how best they can work together in a spirit of determination and common commitment'. It is not, of course, just universities: polytechnics and other institutions of higher education also have a contribution to make. Nevertheless, Rudduck's general point still holds: the notion of an educational community that can facilitate and to some extent resource 'a shared commitment to clarifying values, principles and purposes, and to understanding the social and political contexts in which those values, principles and purposes are set to work' is of paramount importance.

In helping to create such a community, teachers would not only be developing a version of professionalism which relied on something other than either the appeal to teacher autonomy or the claims of externally imposed accountability. They would also be claiming for themselves a future role in the middle ground of educational management: the as yet largely unmapped, and still highly contested, terrain between centre and periphery. To that extent the notion of 'interdependent professional' denotes a significant departure.

Looking forward

'Beginning is not only a kind of action,' wrote Edward Said (1985: xv); 'it is also a frame of mind, a kind of work, an attitude, a consciousness'. To begin to evaluate is not, then, just a matter of initiating certain procedures; it is a matter also of creating a certain kind of context and asking certain kinds of questions. Among the questions that schools, in concert with their professional partners, will need to address in making such a start, are the following:

- What is educational about educational evaluation?
- What conditions must be met before evaluation can fairly claim to be educational?
- What constraints operate against educational evaluation and by what means, if any, can these be overcome?
- What values inform and sustain it?

These, of course, are not the only questions that need to be considered. But they are some of the most important. Starting from these, any school could begin to develop a clear perspective on evaluation and to communicate that perspective to other schools and professional groups. They are pitched at a high level of generality as a reminder that behind the technical, procedural and managerial issues so often associated with evaluation, lie some very big questions about values and purposes.

The preceding chapters, though not addressing these questions directly, were certainly prompted by them and could be read as a response to them. It might be useful, therefore, by way of conclusion, to make explicit that response: not in order to have the last word, but rather to offer some starting points whereby schools can begin to define for themselves what it is that is educational about educational evaluation and, in so doing, develop a common approach to evaluation:

- Educational evaluation is necessarily collegial in spirit. It is the means by which the teaching profession tries to understand and improve its own practice in the light of those values which it espouses. While it may enable schools to become more accountable, it must be distinguished from existing forms of appraisal which have been managerially inspired and are bureaucratically imposed.
- It focuses primarily on the quality of teaching and learning and on the impact of these activities across a wide range of pupil achievement. Although clearly addressing the concerns of policy makers as well as practitioners, it must be distinguished from approaches to evaluation which focus exclusively on policy matters.
- It must also be distinguished from those approaches which, often for the purposes of financial auditing, seek to measure quality solely in terms of outcome indicators. Educational evaluation is concerned with both pedagogical and organizational processes, with unpre-specified as well as pre-specified outcomes, and with the conditions pertaining within particular institutional settings.

- Educational evaluation is research based; which is to say that the insights it offers are grounded in evidence that has been gathered systematically and analysed according to procedures that can be made explicit. In that respect it differs from consultancy or advice, whose authority may be based solely on the wisdom of experience. Insofar as it invites critical response, refutation and modification, it is a form neither of polemic nor of special pleading. Its authority resides in the evidence it brings to bear and in its analysis of that evidence.
- It can, on occasion, be a means of highlighting hidden constraints and contradictions and thereby challenging received opinion regarding the nature or parameters of particular problems. In so doing it can encourage individuals and groups to rethink their own and others' assumptions and to reconceive the possibilities that are open to them. It can, in that sense, be said to fulfil both a critical and an emancipatory function.

The National Curriculum may, in retrospect, be seen to have reinforced the derogatory sense of 'common': prove, that is, to be less about commonality and sharing than about social division; less about entitlement than about the further subordination of what Raymond Williams (1976: 61) characterized as that already 'large specific and subordinate group'. It is, after all, for all its interventionism, part of a legislative package that is strung together with 'the privatiser's market ideology' (Lawton 1989: 38).

This gloomy prognosis is less likely to prove reliable, however, if schools adopt an approach to evaluation which takes as its point of departure the need for teachers to go on thinking, together, about the processes of teaching and learning and about the contexts which frame and constrain these processes. Such departures, as Said (1985: 30) again reminds us, are not easy: 'in the realm of thought, beginning is not really a beginner's game'. It remains, nevertheless, the only game that matters to those for whom evaluation is nothing if not educational.

Summary

What is at stake here is, quite simply, the whole curriculum: the coherence and integrity of what is offered to young people by way of their entitlement to a broad and balanced education. Insofar as 'curriculum coherence . . . is concerned with the way the curriculum hangs together *in the experience of pupils'* (Hargreaves 1987: 9), it relies on immense flexibility and adaptability on behalf of teachers, on a policy framework which encourages long-term planning by schools and on resource levels which allow for real management choices across a range of options. Where 'the structure created to ensure its efficient delivery is rigid and inflexible' (Kelly 1990: 67), the chances of any curriculum meeting the needs of individual pupils – of connecting with their own lives and histories – are slim.

If schools are to tackle seriously the problem of curriculum coherence, teachers will need to take those kinds of connections very seriously. In so doing, however, they will inevitably have to challenge many of the presuppositions of the current policy framework within which schools currently operate. A collegial approach to evaluation will undoubtedly help in this task. In its emphasis on shared enquiry and open dialogue, it must, even if only by implication, counter the insidious drift towards a competitive free for all in which each school is out for itself. Against that demeaning norm, evaluation may prove to be one of the ways in which schools continue to exert a civilizing, and deeply educative, influence.

Bibliography

Adelman, C. (ed.) (1981). *Uttering, Muttering: Collecting, Using and Reporting Talk for Social and Educational Research*. London, Grant McIntyre.

Alkin, M.C. (1987). 'Evaluation – who needs it? Who cares?', in R. Murphy and H. Torrance (eds), *Evaluating Education: Issues and Methods*. London, Paul Chapman.

Alkin, M.C., Daillak, R. and White, P. (1979). *Using Evaluations: Does Evaluation Make a Difference?* London, Sage Publications.

Armstrong, M. (1980). *Closely Observed Children*. London, Writers and Readers.

Armstrong, M. (1981). 'The case of Louise and the painting of landscape', in J. Nixon (ed.), *A Teachers Guide to Action Research*. London, Grant McIntyre.

Audit Commission (1989). *Assuring Quality in Education: The Role of LEA Inspectors and Advisers*. London, HMSO.

Awbrey, M.J. (1989). 'A teacher's action research study in a kindergarten: accepting the natural expression of children', *Peabody Journal of Education* 64 (2): 33–64.

Barnes, D., Johnson, G., Jordan, S. *et al.* (1987a). *The TVEI Curriculum 14–16: An Interim Report Based on Case Studies in Twelve Schools*. School of Education, University of Leeds.

Barnes, D., Johnson, G., Jordan, S. *et al.* (1987b). *A Second Report on the TVEI Curriculum: Courses for 14–16 Year Olds in Twenty-Six Schools*. School of Education, University of Leeds.

Barnes, D., Johnson, G., Jordon, S. *et al.* (1989). *A Third Report on the TVEI Curriculum: Courses for 16–18 Year Olds in*

Sixteen Local Authorities. School of Education, University of Leeds.

Bates, S. (1990). 'A crumbling right wing revolution born of revenge or a guilty conscience', *Guardian* 23 November.

Beattie, N. (1990). 'The wider context: are curricula manageable?', in T. Brighouse and B. Moon (eds), *Managing the National Curriculum: Some Critical Perspectives*. Harlow, Longman/BEMAS.

Bell, L. (1988). 'Appraisal and the search for accountability', in L. Bell (ed.), *Appraising Teachers in Schools*. London, Routledge.

Benn, T. (1989). *Against the Tide (Diaries 1973–76)*. London, Hutchinson.

Berger, J. and Mohr, J. (1969). *A Fortunate Man: The Story of a Country Doctor*. Harmondsworth, Penguin.

Berger, J. and Mohr, J. (1975). *A Seventh Man: The Story of a Migrant Worker in Europe*. Harmondsworth, Penguin.

Berger, J. and Mohr, J. (1982). *Another Way of Telling*. London, Writers and Readers.

Bridgewood, A. (1989). *Working Together: Consortium Links in TVEI* (An evaluation report prepared for the Training Agency). Slough, NFER.

Brighouse, T. and Moon, B. (eds) (1990). *Managing the National Curriculum: Some Critical Perspectives*. Harlow, Longman/BEMAS.

Brighouse, T. and Hunter, P. (1990). 'Too clever by half', *Times Educational Supplement* 6 April.

Broadfoot, P. (1988). 'Records of achievement and the national curriculum framework'. Paper presented at a BERA conference on bench-mark testing (Institute of Education, University of London), 11 February.

Broadfoot, P. (1990). 'Towards curssessment: the symbiotic relationship between curriculum and assessment', in N. Entwistle (ed.), *Handbook of Educational Ideas and Practices*. London, Routledge.

Burgess, R.G. (ed.) (1989). *The Ethics of Educational Research*. Lewes, Falmer Press.

Byrne, E.M. (1974). *Planning and Educational Inequality: A Study of the Rationale of Resource-Allocation*. Slough, NFER.

Carr, W. (ed.) (1989). *Quality in Teaching: Arguments for a Reflective Profession*. London, Falmer Press.

Carr, W. and Kemmis, S. (1986). *Becoming Critical*. London, Falmer Press.

CCCS (1981). *Unpopular Education: Schooling and Social Democracy in England Since 1944*. London, Hutchinson (in association with CCCS).

Challis, M., Davidson, P., Geadell, D., *et al.* (1986). *Pupil Tracking*. Herries School, Sheffield.

Chitty, C. (1986). 'TVEI: the MSC's trojan horse', in C. Benn and J. Farley (eds), *Challenging the MSC*. London, Pluto Press.

CIPFA (1986). *Performance Indicators in the Education Service: a*

Statement. London, Chartered Institute of Public Finance and Accountancy.

CIPFA (1988). *Performance Indicators in Schools: A Contribution to the Debate.* London, Chartered Institute of Public Finance and Accountancy.

Clarke, K. (1990). 'Teacher appraisal to be compulsory', *DES News* 389/90, 10 December.

Clarke, K. (1991). Speech to the North of England Education Conference at Leeds, 4 January.

Clifford, J. (1986). 'Partial truths', in J. Clifford and G.E. Marcus (eds), *Writing Culture: The Poetics and Politics of Ethnography.* California, University of California Press.

Clifford, J. and Marcus, G.E. (eds) (1986). *Writing Culture: The Poetics and Politics of Ethnography.* California, University of California Press.

Clough, E. and Clough, P. (1989). 'Learning, curriculum and assessment: the new balance', in E. Clough, P. Clough and J. Nixon (eds), *The New Learning: Contexts and Futures for Curriculum Reform.* Basingstoke, Macmillan.

Clough, E., Clough, P. and Nixon, J. (eds) (1989). *The New Learning: Contexts and Futures for Curriculum Reform.* Basingstoke, Macmillan.

Clough, P. and Nixon, J. (1989). 'The context of change', in E. Clough, P. Clough and J. Nixon (eds), *The New Learning: Contexts and Futures for Curriculum Reform.* Basingstoke, Macmillan.

Cohen, L. and Manion, L. (1980). *Research Methods in Education.* London, Croom Helm.

Cohen, P. (1984). 'Against the new vocationalism', in I. Bates, J. Clarke, P. Cohen, *et al.* (eds), *Schooling for the Dole?.* Basingstoke, Macmillan.

Coopers and Lybrand (1988). *Local Management of Schools.* London, HMSO.

Corey, S. (1953). *Action Research to Improve School Practice.* New York, Teachers College, Columbia University.

Croll, P. (1986). *Systematic Classroom Observation.* London, Falmer Press.

Denzin, N.K. (1970). *The Research Act in Sociology.* London, Butterworth.

DES (1983). *Teaching Quality.* London, HMSO.

DES (1985a). *Better Schools.* London, HMSO.

DES (1985b). *Quality in Schools: Evaluation and Appraisal.* London, HMSO.

DES (1988a). *National Curriculum: Task Group on Assessment and Testing* (TGAT Report). London, HMSO.

DES (1988b). *Performance Indicators for Secondary Schools: Some Practical Considerations* (a discussion paper). London, DES.

DES (1989). *School Teacher Appraisal: A National Framework*. Report of the National Steering Group on the School Teacher Appraisal Pilot Study. London, HMSO.

Dennison, B. (1990). 'Jobs for the middlemen', *Times Educational Supplement* 19 October.

Dockrell, W.B. and Hamilton, D. (eds) (1980). *Rethinking Educational Research*. London, Hodder and Stoughton.

Eisner, E. (1985). *The Art of Educational Evaluation*. London, Falmer Press.

Elliott, J. (1978). 'Classroom accountability and the self-monitoring teacher', in W. Harlen (ed.), *Evaluation and the Teacher's Role*. Schools Council Research Studies, Basingstoke, Macmillan.

Elliott, J., Bridges, D., Ebbutt, D. *et al*. (1981). *School Accountability* (The SSRC Cambridge Accountability Project). London, Grant McIntyre.

Entwistle, N. (ed.) (1990). *Handbook of Educational Ideas and Practices*. London, Routledge.

Eraut, M., Pennycuick, D. and Radnor, H. (undated). *Local Evaluation of INSET: A Meta-Evaluation of TRIST Evaluations*. University of Sussex.

Evans, A. (1989). 'Leave it to the experts', *Times Educational Supplement* 8 December: 24.

Fitz-Gibbon, C.T. (1990). 'Analysing examination results', in C.T. Fitz-Gibbon (ed.), *Performance Indicators*. BERA Dialogues 2. Clevedon, PA, Multilingual Matters.

Fitz-Gibbon, C.T. (ed.) (1990). *Performance Indicators*, BERA Dialogues 2. Clevedon, PA, Multilingual Matters.

Flanders, N. (1970). *Analysing Teacher Behaviour*. Reading, MA, Addison-Wesley.

Fletcher, N. (1990). 'The Education Reform Act and educational politics', in R. Morris (ed.), *Central and Local Control of Education after the Education Reform Act 1988*. Harlow, Longman/BEMAS.

Fogelman, K. (1990). *Citizenship in Secondary Schools: A National Survey*, Summary report prepared for the Speaker's Commission on Citizenship.

Ford Teaching Project (1975). *Unit 1: Patterns of Teaching; Unit 2: Research Methods; Unit 3: Hypotheses; Unit 4: Teacher Case Studies*. Cambridge, Cambridge Institute of Education.

Galton, M. (1978). *British Mirrors: A Collection of Classroom Observation Instruments*. University of Leicester, School of Education.

Gamble, R. (1990). 'Performance indicators', in C.T. Fitz-Gibbon (ed.), *Performance Indicators*. BERA Dialogues 2. Clevedon, PA, Multilingual Matters.

Giddens, A. (1985). 'Jürgen Habermas', in Q. Skinner (ed.), *The Return of Grand Theory in the Human Sciences*. Cambridge, Cambridge University Press.

Gillborn, D. (1990). 'Sexism and curricular "choice" ', *Cambridge Journal of Education* 20 (2): 161–74.

Gillborn, D., Nixon, J. and Rudduck, J. (1989). Teachers' experiences and perceptions of discipline in ten inner-city comprehensive schools in DES, *Discipline in Schools* (The Elton Report). London, HMSO.

Grace, G. (1987), 'Teachers and the state', in M. Lawn and G. Grace, *Teachers: The Culture and Politics of Work*. Lewes, Falmer Press.

Graham, D. (1990a). Interviewed by Judith Judd, *Independent Sunday* 6 May.

Graham, D. (1990b). 'The wealth of nations', *Times Educational Supplement* 16 November.

Gray, J. (1982). *Making More Sense of Examination Results*. Milton Keynes, Open University Press.

Gray, J. (1990). 'The quality of schooling: frameworks for judgement', *British Journal of Educational Studies* 38 (3): 204–23.

Gray, J., Jesson, D. and Sime, N. (1990). 'Estimating differences in the examination performances of secondary schools in six LEAs: a multi-level approach to school effectiveness', *Oxford Review of Education* 16 (2): 137–58.

Habermas, J. (1970). 'Towards a theory of communicative competence', *Inquiry*, 13 (4): 360–76.

Halsey, A.H. (1986). *Change in British Society*. Oxford, Oxford University Press (third edition).

Halsey, A.H., Heath, A.F. and Ridge, J.M. (1980). *Origins and Destinations: Family, Class and Education in Modern Britain*. Oxford, Oxford University Press.

Hamilton, D. (1976). *Curriculum Evaluation*, London, Open Books.

Hamilton, D. (1990). *Learning about Education: An Unfinished Curriculum*. Milton Keynes, Open University Press.

Hamilton, D., Jenkins, D., King, C., *et al.* (eds) (1977). *Beyond the Numbers Game*. London, Macmillan Education.

Hargreaves, A. (1989). *Curriculum and Assessment Reform*. Milton Keynes, Open University Press.

Hargreaves, D.H. (1982). *The Challenge for the Comprehensive School: Culture, Curriculum and Community*. London, Routledge and Kegan Paul.

Hargreaves, D.H. (1987). 'The quest for school curriculum: directions and destinations', *School Science Review* 69 (246): 7–16.

Hargreaves, D.H. (1990). 'Planting coherence in secret gardens', *Times Educational Supplement* 26 January.

Harland, J. and Sumner, R. (1989). 'The feasibility of local evaluation in the PI era?', Paper presented at the NFER Evaluation for the Nineties Conference, Christ Church, Oxford.

Harlen, W. (ed.) (1978). *Evaluation and the Teacher's Role*. Schools Council Research Studies. Basingstoke, Macmillan.

Harlen, W. and Elliott, J. (1982). 'A checklist for planning or reviewing an evaluation', in R. McCormick, J. Bynner, P. Clift *et al. Calling Education to Account*. London, Heinemann, in association with Open University Press.

Hazelwood, R.D. (1990). 'Attitudes as performance indicators', in C.T. Fitz-Gibbon (ed.), *Performance Indicators*, BERA Dialogues 2. Clevedon, PA, Multilingual Matters.

HMI (1989). *Education Observed 13: Attendance at School*. London, DES.

Hodgson, C. (1990). *Getting Started on Evaluation Projects*. Barnsley LEA/Training Agency.

Holly, P., James, T. and Young, J. (1987). *The Experience of TRIST: Practitioners' Views of INSET and Recommendations for the Future*. London, MSC.

House, E.R. (1980). *Evaluating with Validity*. London, SAGE Publications.

Hopkins, D. (1989). *Evaluation for School Development*. Milton Keynes, Open University Press.

Joseph, K. (1984). Speech to the North of England Education Conference at Sheffield 6 January.

Joseph, K. (1985). Speech to the North of England Education Conference at Chester 4 January.

Kelly, A.V. (1990). *The National Curriculum: A Critical Review*. London, Paul Chapman.

Lawn, M. and Grace, G. (1987). *Teachers: The Culture and Politics of Work*. Lewes, Falmer Press.

Lawton, D. (1989). *The National Curriculum*, in D. Lawton (ed.), *The Education Reform Act: Choice and Control*. London, Hodder and Stoughton.

Lawton, D. (ed.) (1989). *The Education Reform Act: Choice and Control*. London, Hodder and Stoughton.

Lawton, D. and Chitty, C. (eds) (1988). *The National Curriculum*. Bedford Way Papers No. 33. Institute of Education, University of London.

McCormick, R. and James, M. (1983). *Curriculum Evaluation in Schools*. London, Croom Helm.

McCormick, R., Bynner, J., Clift, P. *et al.* (eds) (1982). *Calling Education to Account*. London, Heinemann, in association with Open University Press.

MacDonald, B. (1976). 'Evaluation and the control of education', in D. Tawney (ed.), *Curriculum Evaluation Today: Trends and Implications*. Schools Council Research Studies, Basingstoke, Macmillan.

MacGregor, J. (1990a). Speech to the Society of Education Officers' Conference in London 25 January.

MacGregor, J. (1990b). Interviewed by Jeremy Sutcliffe, *Times Educational Supplement* 16 March.

MacGregor, J. (1990c). Speech to the Assistant Masters and Mistresses Association Conference at Blackpool 9 April.

MacIntyre, A. (1985). *After Virtue: A Study in Moral Theory*, 2nd (corrected) edition (with postscript). London, Duckworth.

McNamara, D. (1990). 'The National Curriculum: an agenda for research', *British Educational Research Journal* 16 (3): 225–35.

Maden, M. (1990). 'Danger in DIY democracy', *Times Educational Supplement* 30 November.

Marcus, G.E. and Fischer, M.J. (1986). *Anthropology as Cultural Critique: An Experimental Moment in the Human Sciences*. Chicago, IL, University of Chicago Press.

May, N. and Sigsworth, A. (1987). 'Teacher-outsider partnerships in the observation of classrooms', in R. Murphy and H. Torrance (eds), *Evaluating Education: Issues and Methods*. London, Paul Chapman.

Mitchell, P. (1984). 'Institutional evaluation: the process within a school', in M. Skilbeck (ed.) *Evaluating the Curriculum in the Eighties*. London, Hodder and Stoughton.

Morrell, F. (1990). 'Rights of passage', *Times Educational Supplement* 2 February.

Morris, R. (ed.) (1990). *Central and Local Control of Education after the Education Reform Act 1988*. Harlow, Longman/BEMAS.

Murphy, R. and Torrance, H. (eds) (1987). *Evaluating Education: Issues and Methods*. London, Paul Chapman.

NCC (1989). *Circular Number 6: The National Curriculum and Whole Curriculum Planning: Preliminary Guidance*. York, NCC.

NCC (1990a). *Curriculum Guidance 3: The Whole Curriculum*. York, NCC.

NCC (1990b). *Curriculum Guidance 4: Education for Economic and Industrial Understanding*. York, NCC.

NCC (1990c). *Curriculum Guidance 8: Education for Citizenship*. York, NCC.

Nebesnuick, D. (1990). *Monitoring and Evaluation and the 1988 Education Reform Act*. Slough, NFER.

Nisbet, J. and Broadfoot, P. (1980). *The Impact of Research on Policy and Practice in Education*. Aberdeen, Aberdeen University Press.

Nixon, J. (ed.) (1981). *A Teachers Guide to Action Research*. London, Grant McIntyre.

Nixon, J. (ed.) (1982). *Drama and the Whole Curriculum*. London, Hutchinson.

Nixon, J. (1985). *A Teacher's Guide to Multicultural Education*. Oxford, Basil Blackwell.

Nixon, J. (ed.) (1987). *Curriculum Change: The Sheffield Experience* (USDE Papers in Education). University of Sheffield Division of Education.

Nixon, J. (1988). 'Evaluation the morning after: living with lost value virginity', *Evaluation and Research in Education* 3 (1): 101–7.

Nixon, J. (1989a). 'What is evaluation after the MSC?' *British Journal of Educational Studies* 37 (2): 125–35 (reprinted in R.G. Burgess (ed.) (1989)). *The Ethics of Educational Research*. Lewes, Falmer Press.

Nixon, J. (1989b). 'Curriculum evaluation: towards the vanishing point', *Westminster Studies in Education* 12: 91–8.

Nixon, J. (1989c). *School-Focused In-Service Education: An Approach to Staff Development*. Basingstoke, Macmillan.

Nixon, J. (1990). 'What is educational about educational evaluation?', *Westminster Studies in Education* 13: 13–20.

Nixon, J., Magee, F. and Sheard, D. (1979). *Teachers in Research*, A report on the Role of the Teacher in Research conference held at Fircroft College, Birmingham, 16–19 November 1979. London, Schools Council.

Nixon, J. and Watts, M. (eds) (1989). *INSET Workshops for Schools: 1. A Whole School Policy for Health & Sex Education*; 2. *Whole School Approaches to Multicultural Education*; 3. *Developing an Equal Opportunities Policy on Gender* (with E.M. O'Brien); 4. *Vocational Aspects of Learning: Towards a Whole School Policy*. (with E.M. O'Brien). Basingstoke, Macmillan.

Nuttall, D., Goldstein, H., Prosser, R. *et al.* (1989). 'Differential school effectiveness', *International Journal of Educational Research* 13: 769–76.

O'Connor, A. (1989). *Raymond Williams: Writing, Culture, Politics*. Oxford, Basil Blackwell.

O'Hear, A. (1990). 'Why Mrs Thatcher must keep in touch', *Times Educational Supplement* 4 May.

Parlett, M. and Hamilton, D. (1977). 'Evaluation as illumination: a new approach to the study of innovation', in D. Hamilton and others, *Beyond the Numbers Game*. London, Macmillan Education.

Powney, J. and Watts, M. (1987). *Interviewing in Educational Research*. London, Routledge and Kegan Paul.

PRAISE (1987). 'Ethical guidelines', in R. Murphy and H. Torrance (eds), *Evaluating Education: Issues and Methods*, London, Paul Chapman.

Pratt, J., Bloomfield, J. and Seale, C. (1984). *Option Choice: A Question of Equal Opportunity*, a study sponsored by the Equal Opportunities Commission. Windsor, NFER Nelson.

Pring, R. (1987). 'Confidentiality and the right to know', in R. Murphy and H. Torrance (eds), *Evaluating Education: Issues and Methods*. London, Paul Chapman.

Ribbins, P. (1990). 'Teachers as professionals: towards a redefinition', in R. Morris (ed.) *Central and Local Control of Education after the Education Reform Act 1988*. Harlow, Longman/BEMAS.

Rizvi, F. and Kemmis, S. (1987). *Dilemmas of Reform: An Overview of*

Issues and Achievements of the Participation and Equity Program in Victorian Schools 1984–86. Deakin Institute for Studies in Education, Deakin University.

Roche, M. (1987). 'Citizenship, social theory and social change', *Theory and Society* 16: 363–99.

Rorty, R. (1989). *Contingency, Irony and Solidarity.* Cambridge, Cambridge University Press.

Rudduck, J. (1976). 'Dissemination as "acculturation research" ', *SSRC Newsletter* 32: 7–10.

Rudduck, J. (1978). 'Dissemination as the encounter of cultures', *Research Intelligence* 3 (1): 3–5.

Rudduck, J. (1986a). 'Curriculum change: management or meaning?', *School Organisation* 6 (1): 107–14.

Rudduck, J. (1986b). *Understanding Curriculum Change*, USDE Papers in Education. Division of Education, University of Sheffield.

Rudduck, J. (1991). *Innovation and Change.* Milton Keynes, Open University Press.

Rudduck, J. and Wilcox, B. (1988). 'Issues of ownership and partnership in school-centred innovation: the Sheffield experience', *Research Papers in Education* 3 (3): 157–79.

Rustin, M. (1989). 'The politics of post-Fordism: or, the trouble with "new times" ', *New Left Review* 175: 54–77.

Said, E.W. (1985). *Beginnings: Intention and Method.* New York, Columbia University Press.

Sayer, J. (1989). *Managing Schools.* London, Hodder and Stoughton.

Schön, D. (1987). *Educating the Reflective Practitioner.* London, Jossey-Bass.

SCIA (1989). *Evaluating the Achievements of Schools and Colleges. Performance Indicators in Perspective.* London, Society of Chief Inspectors and Advisers.

Shipman, M. (1979). *In-School Evaluation.* London, Heinemann.

Shumsky, A. (1956). 'Co-operation in action research: a rationale', *Journal of Educational Sociology* 30: 180–5.

Shumsky, A. (1958). 'The personal significance of action research', *Journal of Teacher Education* 9: 152–5.

Sime, N. (1991). *Sixteen and Seventeen Year Olds in the Late Eighties.* Sheffield, Training Agency.

Simon, A. and Boyer, G. (1970). *Mirrors for Behaviour, Vols I and II.* Philadelphia, PA, Research for Better Schools.

Simon, A. and Boyer, G. (1974). *Mirrors for Behaviour, Vol. III.* Philadelphia, PA, Research for Better Schools.

Simons, H. (1981). 'Conversation piece: the practice of interviewing in case study research', in C. Adelman (ed.) *Uttering, Multering: Collecting, Using and Reporting Talk for Social and Educational Research.* London, Grant McIntyre.

Simons, H. (1987). *Getting to Know Schools in a Democracy: The Politics and Process of Evaluation*. Lewes, Falmer Press.

Simons, H. (1989). 'Ethics of case study in educational research and evaluation', in R.G. Burgess (ed.) *The Ethics of Educational Research*. Lewes, Falmer Press.

Skilbeck, M. (ed.) (1984). *Evaluating the Curriculum in the Eighties*. London, Hodder and Stoughton.

Smith, D. and Tomlinson, S. (1989). *The School Effect: A study of Multiracial Comprehensives*. London, Policy Studies Institute.

Stenhouse, L. (1975). *An Introduction to Curriculum Research and Development*. London, Heinemann.

Stenhouse, L. (1981). 'Drama as a discipline of thinking', in J. Norman (ed.), *Drama in Education: A Curriculum for Change*, The Report of the 1981 Annual Conference of the National Association for the Teaching of Drama. Banbury, Kemble Press.

Stenhouse, L., Verma, G.K., Wild, R.D. and Nixon, J. (1982). *Teaching about Race Relations: Problems and Effects*. London, Routledge and Kegan Paul.

Stillman, A. and Grant, M. (1989). *The LEA Adviser: A Changing Role*. Windsor, NFER Nelson.

Tawney, D. (ed.) (1976). *Curriculum Evaluation Today: Trends and Implications*. Schools Council Research Studies, Basingstoke, Macmillan.

Thatcher, M. (1990). Interviewed by Trevor Grove, *Sunday Telegraph* 15 April.

Tipple, C. (1989), 'Measuring achievement', *Education* 29 September: 280–1.

Torrance, H. (1987). 'What can examinations contribute to school evaluations?', in R. Murphy and H. Torrance (eds) *Evaluating Education: Issues and Methods*. London, Paul Chapman.

Trethowan, D. (1987). *Appraisal and Target Setting*. London, Harper and Row.

TRIST (1987). *School/College Liaison and the Development of Consortia* (Papers of National Interest 3). London, Training Agency.

TVEI (1988). *Profiles and Records of Achievement*, Developments 5. London, Training Agency.

Valéry, P. (1947). 'Poetry and abstract thought', in J.L. Hevesi, *Essays on Language and Literature*. London, Allan Wingate.

Walker, R. (1980). 'The conduct of educational case studies', in D.W. Dockrell and D. Hamilton (eds), *Rethinking Educational Research*. London, Hodder and Stoughton.

Walker, R. (1985). *Doing Research*. London, Methuen.

Weiss, C.H. and Bucuvalas, M.J. (1980). *Social Science Research and Decision-Making*. New York, Columbia University Press.

Wilcox, B. (1986). 'Context and issues', in Edgar Stones and B. Wilcox (eds), *Appraising Appraisal: A Critical Examination of Proposals for the Appraisal of Teachers in England and Wales*. London, British Educational Research Association.

Wilcox, B. (1989). 'Monitoring for survival', *Education* 24 March: 278.

Wilcox B. (1991a). *Evaluation for LEAs and TECs: Some Guiding Principles*. University of Sheffield, QQSE.

Wilcox, B. (1991b). *Time-Constrained Evaluation: A Practical Approach for LEAs and Schools*. London, Routledge.

Williams, R. (1965). *The Long Revolution*. Harmondsworth, Penguin (first published by Chatto and Windus 1961).

Williams, R. (1970). *The English Novel from Dickens to Lawrence*. London, Chatto and Windus.

Williams, R. (1976). *Key Words*. London, Fontana/Croom Helm.

Williams, R. (1979). *Politics and Letters*. London, New Left Books.

Williams, R. (1980). *Problems in Materialism and Culture: Selected Essays*. London, Verso.

Williams, R. (1989). *Resources of Hope*. London, Verso.

Index

Alkin, M.C., 24, 109, 110
anti-racist teaching, 31
appraisal, 12–14
Armstrong, M., 21
assessment
  examination and test data, 29,
    32, 71–6, 86, 120
  limitations, 67–8
  recent developments, 10–12
attendance data, 71, 76–9, 86
Audit Commission, 122–3
Awbrey, M.J., 34

Baker, K., 12, 13, 54, 122
Barnes, D., 62–4
Bates, S., 119
Beattie, N., 120
Bell, L., 13
Benn, T., 117
Berger, J., 5
Bloomfield, J., 83
Boyer, G., 62
Bridgewood, A., 9
Brighouse, T., 53
Broadfoot, P., 11, 25

Bucuvalas, M., 24
Byrne, E.M., 79

Callaghan, J.
  Ruskin College speech, 117
Carr, W., 22, 29
case study, 43
CCCS, 117
Challis, M., 65–7
Chitty, C., 2
CIPFA, 14, 15
Clarke, K., 13, 82
Classroom Action Research
    Network, 7
Clifford, J., 109
Clough, E., 10
Clough, P., 3, 10
Cohen, L., 87, 99
Cohen, P., 2
collegiality
    as an approach to evaluation,
      21–4, 42, 47, 120, 125, 127
    and the culture of teaching,
      103–4
    links with external agencies, 112
common curriculum, 117–18, 126

Coopers and Lybrand, 9
Corey, S., 7
Croll, P., 62
cross-curriculum 'themes'
  careers education and guidance,
    52
  citizenship, 30, 52, 55–6, 78,
    118
  economic and industrial
    understanding, 2, 25–6, 52,
    56
  environmental education, 52, 55
  health education, 52, 55
curriculum coherence
  as the experience of learning,
    56–8, 65, 82, 127
  and the National Curriculum,
    51–6
  in relation to breadth and
    balance, 83–4
  and research methodology, 87

Daillak, R., 24
Dennison, B., 121–2
Denzin, N.K., 99
destinations of school leavers,
    79–81, 86
Dickens, C., 101
dissemination
  cultural aspects of, 103–4
  external audiences, 112–14
  occasions for, 104–8
  reporting, 108–11

Eisner, E., 5
Elliott, J., 7, 19, 21, 38–9, 40, 46
equal opportunities
  comprehensive schooling, 80
  as a cross-curriculum
    'dimension', 55
  gender bias, 81, 83, 107
  school policy, 27–8
Eraut, M., 37
ethical issues
  access, 46–7

confidentiality, 47–8, 60
  release of data, 47–8
ethnography, 43
Evans, A., 13

fiction, 43, 101, 109
Fischer, M.J., 114
Fitz-Gibbon, C.T., 73
Flanders, N., 62
Fletcher, N., 119, 122
Fogelman, K., 55
Ford Foundation, 6
Ford Teaching Project, 7

Galton, M., 62
Gamble, R., 73
Giddens, A., 23
Gillborn, D., 79, 83
Grace, G., 3
Graham, D., 82
Grant, M., 120
Gray, J., 17, 18, 29, 72, 74–5
Great Debate, 117

Habermas, J., 22
Halsey, A.H., 79–80
Hamilton, D., 4, 5, 99
Hargreaves, A., 33, 34
Hargreaves, D.H., 52, 55, 65, 103
Harland, J., 14
Harlen, W., 38–9, 40, 46
Hazelwood, R., 84
Heath, A.F., 79
HMI, 52, 54, 76–7
Hodgson, C., 65
Holly, P., 37
Hopkins, D., 37
House, E., 48, 50
Humanities Curriculum Project, 7,
    111
Hunter, P., 53

impact
  areas of, 20
  direct, 28–33

indirect, 24–8
wider influence, 33–5
interviews
    analysis of interview data, 98
    'outsider' as interviewer, 92–3
    procedures, 94–8
    with pupils, 89–92
    range of, 87–9
    in relation to other research
        methods, 86, 100
    reporting of, 98

James, M., 108, 112
James, T., 37
Jesson, D., 29
Joseph, K., 12, 13

Kelly, A.V., 127
Kemmis, S., 22

LAPP, 2
Lawrence, D.H., 101
Lawton, D., 126
LEAs
    advisers/inspectors, 9, 43, 48,
        106, 112, 119–20
    curriculum policy, 31
    league tables, 29
    local evaluation, 37
    recent developments, 1, 4, 9,
        11, 121–3
local finance and management of
    schools, 9, 119, 120

McCormick, R., 108, 112
MacDonald, B., 23
MacGregor, J., 13, 54
MacIntyre, A., 22
McNamara, D., 116
Maden, M., 121, 122
Magee, F., 107
Manion, L., 87, 99
Marcus, G.E., 114
May, N., 59
Mitchell, P., 21

Mohr, J., 5
Morrell, F., 56
multicultural education, 31, 55

Nebesnuick, D., 123
Nisbet, J., 25
Nixon, J., 3, 7, 41, 79, 85, 105,
    107
Nuffield Foundation, 6
Nuttall, D., 29

observation, 27, 58–64
O'Connor, A., 103
O'Hear, A., 54
open enrolment, 8–9, 119, 120
opting out, 9, 119, 120

Parlett, M., 5
Pennycuick, D., 37
performance indicators, 14–18, 45
Powney, J., 99–100
Pratt, J., 83
Pring, R., 49
professionalism, 3–4, 18–19,
    34–5, 36, 104, 122–4
progressive focussing, 42–6, 59
pupil tracking, 65–7

questionnaire, 26, 84–5

Radnor, H., 37
records of achievement
    and GCSE coursework, 68
    Northern Partnership for
        Records of Achievement, 11
    Oxford Certificate of
        Educational Achievement, 11
    PRAISE, 48
Ribbins, P., 123
Ridge, J.M., 79
Rizvi, F., 22
Roche, M., 55
Rorty, R., 50

Rudduck, J., 7, 79, 102–3, 111, 124
Rustin, M., 4

Said, E., 124, 126
Sayer, J., 102, 119
Schön, D., 3
Schools Council, 6
SCIA, 12, 14, 15–17
Seale, C., 83
Sheard, D., 107
Shipman, M., 72, 76, 77, 78, 81
Shumsky, A., 7
Sigsworth, A., 59
Sime, N., 29, 75
Simon, A., 62
Simons, H., 21, 49, 90
Smith, D., 29
Stenhouse, L., 7, 92
Stillman, A., 120
Sumner, R., 14

teacher as researcher, 7, 21
Thatcher, M., 54

Thatcherism, 2, 117
Tipple, C., 14
Tomlinson, S., 29
Torrance, H., 76
Trethowan, D., 14
triangulation, 46, 99–100
TRIST, 2, 9, 15, 37
TVEI, 2, 3, 11, 37, 62, 121

Valéry, P., 76

Walker, R., 7, 85, 93
Watts, M., 99–100, 105
Weiss, C., 24
White, P., 24
Wilcox, B., 7, 12, 123
Williams, R., 5, 101–2, 104, 117–18, 126
Williams, S., 117

Young, J., 37